WUTHERING
HEIGHTS

a study

A Note About the Author

U. C. Knoepflmacher, Paton Foundation Professor of Ancient and Modern Literature at Princeton University, has written extensively on nineteenth-century British literature.

WUTHERING
HEIGHTS

a study

U. C. Knoepflmacher

Ohio University Press

Athens

Library of Congress Cataloging-in-Publication Data

Knoepflmacher, U. C.
Wuthering Heights: A study / U. C. Knoepflmacher.
p. cm.
Originally published: Cambridge; New York:
Cambridge University Press, 1989.
Includes bibliographical references and index.
ISBN 0-8214-1078-4 (pbk.)
1. Brontë, Emily, 1818–1848. Wuthering Heights.
I.   Title.
PR4172.W73K58   1994
823'.8–dc20   93-39317
                                                               CIP

Ohio University Press, Athens, Ohio 45701
© 1989 by U. C. Knoepflmacher
Preface to Ohio University Press edition
© 1994 by U. C. Knoepflmacher
Printed in the United States of America

Published by arrangement with Cambridge University Press

Ohio University Press books are printed on acid-free paper ∞

99 98   5 4 3 2

Contents

Preface

Over half a century has elapsed since Laurence Olivier and Merle Oberon grandly acted out the roles of star-crossed lovers on the screen. The lush 1939 film of *Wuthering Heights,* directed by William Wyler, probably did more to reinstate Emily Brontë's masterpiece than any sober reevaluation by literary critics. Virginia Woolf, C. P. Sanger, and Lord David Cecil had already reassessed and significantly revalidated the novel by the time that the Hollywood film appeared (see p. 129, below). Yet the Academy Award-winning cinematography of Gregg Toland, the extravagant musical score by Alfred Newman, and, above all, Olivier's mesmeric performance as Heathcliff surely influenced a public much larger (and also less literary in its outlook) than that affected by the dicta of Bloomsbury intellectuals.

The movie's effect seems to have been quite long-lasting. For many years after its completion, its producer, Samuel Goldwyn, indulged himself by ritually rolling the film over and over again in lachrimose home viewings. But he was hardly alone in weeping at the sights and sounds of the emotive final scene: as Newman's soundtrack reaches a lyrical crescendo, the beautiful ghosts holding hands take their solitary way "with wand'ring steps and slow" through the unquiet heather undulating beneath Penistone Crag. They are at last united, no longer beset by social inequality or hostility. In 1939, Americans who had survived the hardships of the Depression only to find themselves poised on the edge of another world war may have been justifiably drawn towards this escapist closure. It certainly was not the open ending that Brontë had so brilliantly devised. When I show Wyler's film (as well as Luis Buñuel's anti-Hollywood adaptation) after several meetings on Brontë's text, my students cruelly snicker at this sentimental climax. Time passes.

It is difficult to say which of the two major mistakes made by the 1939 film's scriptwriters, Ben Hecht and Charles Mac-Arthur, is the more egregious: their omission of the second generation of lovers who replace Heathcliff and Catherine or their decision to convert Lockwood, Brontë's youthful narrator and narratee, into a bent old man. Yet both of these mistakes actually stem from the selfsame source. For, in adapting Brontë's text for the screen, Hecht and MacArthur chose to deny its central concern with that intermediate state between childhood and maturity that we call adolescence. The extraordinary blending of analytical intelligence and profound sympathy that Emily Brontë brings to bear on adolescence separates this text by the sister whom Yorkshire villagers called "t' cleverest o' t' Brontë childer" from the work of her imaginative siblings. That mixture also significantly links her novel to the Romantic productions of a previous generation.

In his preface to *Endymion,* a poem that was published in 1818, the same year that Emily Brontë was born, John Keats had tried to define adolescence by treating it as a transient mental site or passageway: "The imagination of a boy is healthy, and the mature imagination of a man is healthy; but there is a space of life between, in which the soul is in a ferment, the character undecided, the way of life uncertain." Keats also recognized, however, that such indecision need hardly be a hallmark of artistic immaturity. In letters written around the same time, he allowed that the exploration of the dubious "dark passages" that lie beyond childhood and adolescence was an enterprise worthy of the highest Romantic "genius." And he also claimed that the "quality" of being able to retain "uncertainties, Mysteries, doubts, without any irritable reaching after fact & reason" could, in fact, lead to still higher creative achievements. Instead of mimetically reproducing the indecision or turmoil that mark the egress from the Edens of an unreflecting childhood and a self-absorbed adolescence (phases which Keats places in the first and second chambers of a "Mansion of Many Apartments"), the artist should confront "the burden of the Mystery" by remaining open to irresolution, the insecurity and risk that come by entertaining alternative points of view. Thus, whereas Shakespearean drama persistently entertains contrary outlooks, a Shakespearean critic such as Coleridge strikes Keats as shying away from the "Penetralium of mystery" by demanding certainties that Shakespeare's "Negative Capability" refuses to yield.

Keats, who died at twenty-five before Emily Brontë's third birthday, would have been an ideal reader of *Wuthering Heights*. For her part, although she was an astute reader of Romantic texts by Wordsworth, DeQuincey, and the Shelleys (as I try to show in pp. 26–38 of this study), the extent of Emily Brontë's contact with Keats's own work remains rather uncertain. She would unquestionably have agreed with the ideas about form and meaning he voiced in the letters from which I have just quoted. But since the letters went unpublished until 1848, a year after the appearance of *Wuthering Heights* and the year of her own early death, Brontë could at best have inferred some of these ideas through a familiarity with a few of his poems.

The affinities between *Wuthering Heights* and Keats's theories and practice therefore seem all the more striking. The two poets who had turned from lyrical utterance to ironic and dramatic narratives relied on similar topographies and similar agents in interrogative structures designed to penetrate the unknown: like the youthful speaker of "The Fall of Hyperion" or like Porphyro in "The Eve of St. Agnes," Lockwood stumbles into a primal female space associated with an irreparable fall. No visionary but a mere dreamer, the young man who flees Catherine's oak bed is reluctant to take risks. Yet despite his unwillingness to negotiate his way through dark passages, Lockwood leads the reader into the nook that has acted as a cradle for imaginations more powerful than his. The mental architecture that identifies phases of life with closed chambers and open spaces is as central for a novel named after a building as it is for Keats's verse narratives about entry and egress. Even the language used in describing these unstable mansions of the mind is remarkably similar: if Keats insists on pushing his impetuous young protagonists— Lycius, Porphyro, the Hyperion poet, and the pale and feverish knight who ventures into an alien "grot"—into female spaces that lie past "the Penetralium of mystery," the rushed Lockwood, too, is denied a chance of "inspecting the penetralium" of a mysterious dwelling that lacks any "introductory lobby or passage" to aid his desire for explanation.

Above all, however, *Wuthering Heights* consummately enlists the "Negative Capability" that Keats prized so highly in Shakespeare and tried to embody in his own poetry. Brontë's narrative veils what it reveals; it invites interpretation yet resists the simplifications that its tellers and listeners so fervently desire. Frustrated by the book's clashing points of view and its mixture of emotionalism and irony, some of its original detractors wrongly faulted it for a presumed "coarseness" in execution—the same charge, significantly enough, that had been leveled at Keats's *Endymion* by contemporary reviewers who denied his craftsmanship, decried his lack of education, and derided him as being "only a boy of pretty abilities, which he has done everything in his power to spoil." Even Charlotte Brontë, though ostensibly defending her dead sister's novel in her 1850 preface to a new edition of *Wuthering Heights,* felt compelled to excuse its "rusticity" by attributing its "faults" to the limited imagination of a still immature, "homebred country girl."

Charlotte's portrait of an unrefined writer whose mental growth was cut short by early death curiously resembles what had become a standard caricature of Keats by the 1840s—a feminized and unworldly artist who had died before genuine talents could truly have sprouted. There were personal reasons for Charlotte's reliance on this stereotype. As I try to suggest on pp. 5–10 and 110–15 below, she needed to distance herself from both *Wuthering Heights* and its author. Her identification of Emily with the regressiveness that *Wuthering Heights* so clinically investigates thus has less to do with a balanced estimate of her sister's venturesome art than with Charlotte's resistance to certain "dark passages" in her own creative past. She wanted no light shed on the melodramatic fictions she had shared with her brother Branwell during their late adolescence. Her own novel, *The Professor,* written at the same time that Emily worked on *Wuthering Heights,* was an attempt to exorcise the male adolescent fantasies that had once so immensely appealed to her. In its sympathetic treatment of figures who defy socialization, *Wuthering Heights* reopened, for Charlotte, passages she preferred to see blocked. She did not care to revisit primal spaces. Whereas Catherine and Heathcliff want to recover the quasi-incestual oneness they enjoyed in the seclusion of their oak-panelled enclave, Bertha Mason bites her brother in the attic chamber to which she has been confined.

In her 1850 "Editor's Preface to *Wuthering Heights,*" a document I closely analyze in the opening pages of this study, Charlotte Brontë treats her sister's text with something of the same mixture of fascination and repulsion that Jane Eyre exhibits in her confrontations with her demonic double. But whereas Jane can erase her memories of Bertha Mason as soon as she opts for a life of domesticity, Charlotte is disturbed to find that the imprint left by a creature as capable of "fierce and inhuman" sentiments as Heathcliff cannot be expunged by the domestication of Hareton and the second Catherine. The editor of *Wuthering Heights* thus finds herself compelled to denounce an unexorcisable, Satanic "passion such as might boil and glow in the bad essence of some evil genius." As I note on pp. 9–10 below, it seems hardly coincidental that the defensive and quietistic diction which Charlotte employs at the beginning and end of her 1850 "Editor's Preface" should unconsciously mimic that of Lockwood, whose rhetoric is designed to fend off the inflammatory effect of the passions that rule at the Heights. Interestingly enough, however, Charlotte also relies on images that almost seem taken from the opening stanza of Keats's "To Autumn," that poem about fruition and unfulfillment, in trying to describe a sororal imagination specially attuned to the plight of masculine figures unable or unwilling to reach full maturation. Emily, who acutely empathized with her brother Branwell's

plight, thus is herself presented as a figure whose development has been prematurely stunted. Like Keats, Branwell, or
Spenser's man-tree Fradubio, she can be characterized as an
emblem of unfulfillment: "her mind would of itself have
grown like a strong tree, loftier, straighter, wider-spreading,
and its matured fruits would have attained a mellower
ripeness and sunnier bloom, but on that mind time and experience alone could work."

If even as knowing a reader as Charlotte Brontë could un-
dervalue the maturity of the intelligence that shapes *Wuthering Heights*, it seems hardly surprising that Emily's original
audience, unsettled by the novel's subject matter and by that
subject's representation, should have badly misjudged its sophistication. Yet even in the 1880s, when a new generation
began to regard the book much more favorably, advocates and
admirers continued to distort its mode. Long before the 1939
film encouraged the notion that *Wuthering Heights* was indeed
the hazy "mystical" romance that Emily Brontë was most
careful to avoid, others had tried to soften the brutality its
characters so persistently display. A. C. Swinburne, whose
interest in sado-masochism was far from casual, relied on
several strategies to overcome the aversion of Victorian readers to those "vivid and fearful scenes" that had so badly
rattled Emily's sisters that Charlotte claimed that their impact
"banished sleep by night, and disturbed mental peace by day."

In an 1877 letter to the author of a book on Charlotte
Brontë, Swinburne contended that he had met a rural gentlewoman who remarked that the brutality of *Wuthering Heights*
was hardly exaggerated and that, in fact, "she had known
wilder instances of lawless and law-defying passion and tyr-
anny, far more horrible than any cruelty of Heathcliff's, in
her own immediate neighborhood." Having defended the
novel's brutal scenes for their presumed realism and foundation in fact, Swinburne then adopts a more literary tack by
linking such horror to the cruelties depicted on the Jacobean
stage and in Shelley's *The Cenci*. Lastly, in an important 1883
essay that marked a turning point in the estimation of *Wuthering Heights*, Swinburne appears to have decided that the best

way to reclaim the writer he hailed as a "Titaness" was to
purify her fiction.

Though acknowledging that some of the violent details in
Wuthering Heights may "make the reader feel for a moment as
though he were reading a police report or even a novel by
some French 'naturalist' of the latest and brutallest order,"
Swinburne quickly assures his readers that Emily Brontë was
no Zola: "the pervading atmosphere of the book is so high
and healthy that the effect even of those 'vivid and fearful
scenes' which impaired the rest of Charlotte Brontë is almost
at once neutralized—we may hardly say softened, but sweet-
ened, dispersed, and transfigured—by the general impression
of noble purity and passionate straightforwardness, which removes it at once and for ever from any such ugly possibility
of association or comparison. . . . Not till the story is ended,
not till the effect of it has been thoroughly absorbed and di-
gested, does the reader even perceive the simple and natural
absence of any grosser element. . . . As was the author's life,
so is her book in all things: troubled and taintless." By trying
to make virtues out of the very "faults" that Charlotte Brontë
had sadly claimed to recognize, Swinburne threatens to become just as one-sided in his well-meant defence. Charlotte's
version of a creator "passively" possessed by an ugly "demon life" she could "not always master" is now simply reversed. Emily Brontë has become an author who has managed
to sweeten and transfigure all impurities in a "troubled yet
untainted" construct that somehow mirrors the nobility and
rectitude of her own life.

The criticism of Charlotte Brontë and Swinburne is helpful
in reminding us that *Wuthering Heights* can easily seduce professedly impartial interpreters into violating the text's "Negative Capability." Drawn to the novel's psycho-sexual and so-
cioeconomic dynamics, our own generation of gender-critics
and Marxist theorists has not been immune to the temptation
of indulging some of the extravagant inferences that Brontë's
narrative simultaneously encourages and resists. The novel's
reliance on foils and obstacles is integral to its longing for an
erosion of the barriers it dramatizes. Brontë introduces all the

opposites through which we have learned to define our self-
hood: child and adult, female and male, the irrational and the
rational, classlessness and classboundedness, play and power,
free will and determinism. She implants her own dualities by
alternating between two localities, two families, two narrators, two timeschemes; and she intersplices comedy and
tragedy, myth and history, the pastoral and the urban, dream
and common sense. Yet like Keats and like Shakespeare, she
never upholds one polarity over its counterpart, nor dissolves
contraries into some synthesis. By refusing to resolve the dramatic conflicts that fuel her narrative, she compels us to take
a fresh look at those elementary acts of relation which mark
our identity as social—or as asocial—human beings.

This study of *Wuthering Heights* examines the various kinds
of structure that we must dismantle and reassemble before we
can even begin to assign "meanings" to Emily Brontë's elusive text. My own four-part structure mirrors, in a way, the
progress followed by readers of *Wuthering Heights*. That progress is anticipated in the two chronological tables that precede
my actual discussion: whereas the first of these tables situates
the book's author within the political and cultural history of
the nineteenth century, the second one charts the intercon-
nected chronologies to which we are subjected as soon as we
have entered her narrative. That entrance is carefully analyzed in the first chapter. Here, too, the movement is from
an outward actuality to a fictional inner space. After a brief
consideration of the cultural climate of 1850, the Victorian
"noon" that Charlotte, but not Emily, was allowed to reach, I
look at the two essays which the sister-editor placed in the
way of any Victorian reader willing to push, like Lockwood,
beyond barriers that seemed both forbidding and inviting.
After entering with Lockwood into the text, I spend considerable time on his attempts to decode the "Mysteries" on which
he has stumbled. Despite his shortcomings, this curious
young man acts as the reader's prime agent. Lockwood's frag-
ile masculinity, which accounts for his sexual insecurity and
contributes to his defensive maneuvers, also makes him un-
usually receptive to the feminine, to the asocial energies of

the child, and, potentially at least, to the plight of the lovers who so desperately try to recover the androgynous oneness of their earlier life. As I try to show in the last section of this opening chapter, the "sympathetic chord" which Lockwood ultimately denies to Heathcliff and to the second Catherine links this would-be Romantic to the problematics of Romantic sympathy that Emily Brontë well understood from her readings of DeQuincey and the Shelleys.

My second chapter turns to Brontë's management of her complex narrative after Lockwood's hasty exit from the violated shell of Catherine's bed. Lockwood's exile from that "oak case" marks his and our submission to a better-informed narrator, the "sensible" Nelly Dean, who now becomes the prime manager of the novel's narrative rhythms. These rhythms, however, are never wholly controlled by one whose own identifications and sympathies often remain suspect. Voices other than Lockwood's and Nelly's are needed to create a counter-narration that defies the editorializing of these two characters as much as the polyphony of *Wuthering Heights* itself defies the rigidifying editorial frame imposed by Charlotte Brontë. Thus, as I note at one point, it seems significant that well before the voice of a "steady" and sober adult begins to dominate the account of the Earnshaw and Linton families, we should already have had access to the defiant voice of a rebellious girl on the verge of puberty. The still "unknown Catherine" establishes her authority in the diary entries that Lockwood and the reader are allowed to process before the steadiness of Mrs. Dean's narrative helps to compose Lockwood's inflamed imagination. Catherine's *ur*-text remains a rallying point throughout all the later twists and turns of the plot. Nelly Dean may dismiss the young woman who is about to bear a child as being herself "no better than a wailing child." For her part, Catherine derides this older rival as a "withered hag" with gray hair and "bent shoulders," the Blakean emblem of a sterile Experience. And she persists in wishing herself "a girl again, half savage and hardy." Nelly never discovers that this retrogressive wish has actually been fulfilled in Lockwood's second dream. There, the visitor who uses her married name took the shape of a wailing phantom-child in trying to reclaim the bed she had shared with Heathcliff before the onset of their puberty and gender-bifurcation. Catherine's resistance of sexual maturation will eventually be embraced by the potent Heathcliff. This masculine sadist—from whose "man's shape animated by demon life" Charlotte Brontë recoiled far more violently than from Jane's "master" Rochester—undergoes a gender-reversal of sorts at the end of the novel. By succeeding in his self-starvation, he carries to its farthest extreme Catherine's own anorectic attempts to reverse the process of maturation.

Chapter three builds on the previous discussion by confronting at long last the "meanings" encased within Brontë's concentric structures. I begin by considering Nelly, Heathcliff, and Lockwood as interpreters of the myth of a sexual fall conveyed by the story of Catherine's disillusion with her empowerment. At first, Nelly and Heathcliff become competitors in a power-struggle of their own: although they ostensibly fight over the grandchildren of the patriarch who had brought both of them to the Heights, they symbolically enact the conflict in allegiances that destroyed Catherine. Nelly's final empowerment as godmother of her grownup nurslings converts her into something like the "presiding genius" over "home and heart" that Lockwood had vainly sought at the Heights. Yet her pleasure in presiding over the maturation of Hareton and the second Catherine is offset by Heathcliff's own intense delight in rejecting an order of reality ruled by power politics and sexual domination. This conflict between two antagonistic orders of reality, identified with the contrary satisfaction of the freedoms offered by childplay and of the powers that come with adult sexuality, was anticipated, early in the novel, by the marked difference that separates the two dreams Lockwood experienced in Catherine's and Heathcliff's oak-panelled bed. After closely analyzing, at long last, these two dreams, I speculate about Lockwood's overreaction and ask why Brontë should feel compelled to involve us in his mechanisms of repression. The oak bed, I propose, conceals something as terrifying as the Red Room in *Jane Eyre*. In adopting Lockwood's defensiveness in her own "Editor's Preface," Charlotte Brontë possibly responded to the transgressive possibilities opened by a sororal text that relies on a repetitive patterning of brother-sister relations.

These relations may well involve more than Catherine/Hindley, Edgar/Isabella, or those siblings once-removed, the cousins Cathy/Linton and Cathy/Hareton. Nelly, who regards Hindley as a brother, and Heathcliff, who views Catherine as a self-extension, may have a claim on consanguinity if they are the illegitimate offspring of the brooding patriarch on whose protection they originally depended. Yet whether or not the novel flirts with incestual taboos, *Wuthering Heights* does call attention to the passions of repulsion and attraction that shape the early relations among competing siblings. It seems significant that the tempestuous fraternal and sororal relations that Charlotte Brontë tried to elide by making Jane Eyre an only child are much more openly evident in Emily's text. The passionate "play" that Branwell Brontë introduced at Haworth and continued to share with his aroused sisters continued well into late adolescence. Emily Brontë was far more sympathetic to the pathos of Branwell's arrested adolescence than either Charlotte or Anne allowed themselves to be. By considering the role that this fraternal figure may indirectly play in *Wuthering Heights*, I take my readers back to an external world. Yet the coordinates provided by what lies outside of the novel can only be partially trusted, as the Branwellian Lockwood discovers when he flees the inner recesses of the Heights.

Wuthering Heights ends as inconclusively as it began. Lockwood's insistence on a quietistic closure jars with the testimony of the little Blakean shepherd boy. As chapter four tries to illustrate, Brontë's unsettled ending helped to stimulate later artists in creating constructs that address the contraries she identified and kept in suspension. My last chapter distinguishes the reworkings of Emily's novel by fellow-Victorians—her sisters Anne and Charlotte in *The Tenant of Wildfell Hall* and *Villette*, respectively, and George Eliot and Matthew Arnold—from even more radical twentieth-century reformulations. Brontë's special appeal to modernists may lie, as L. P. Hartley has suggested, in her anticipation of a world that witnessed the total breakdown of the civilities which the Victorians still took for granted or to which they at least could pay lip service. Although *Wuthering Heights* had an un-questionable impact on the novels of Hardy and Lawrence, I prefer to consider the book's "after-life" in other media. I therefore look at the Brontëan "relations" embedded in Bal-thus's 1937 painting "Les Enfants" and at Luis Buñuel's de-liberate subversion, in the 1953 film *Abismos de Pasión*, of the sentimentalities that produced Samuel Goldwyn's tears. The identification with Brontë by two artists who are pre-eminently identified with French surrealism seems hardly co-incidental; Brontëan irony also resurfaces, after all, in Fran-çois Truffaut's *Jules et Jim*, as I suggest in the last paragraphs of my study. In his sophisticated critique of Romanticism, Truffaut looks askance at the Rousseauvian notion that the sexual passions of adolescence can propel humans from self-love to a wider love of their kind. The "second birth" of ado-lescence that Rousseau had hailed in *Émile* becomes, in Truffaut's handling, a self-destructive and nihilistic passion that devours his Catherine and Jim far more cruelly than the sexual-yet-desexualized desire that had engulfed Brontë's Catherine and Heathcliff.

*   *   *

This new preface affords me an opportunity to express my gratitude to earlier readers who went unthanked before. I shall never be able to match or repay James Kincaid for his careful page-by-page annotations of my original manuscript. He helped me clarify my thoughts and refine their expression, as did—at a later stage—both Trudi Tate and Linda Shires. I owe a special thanks to Professor Tess Cosslett of Lancaster University. Her enthusiastic review of the book after its pub-lication in England was all the more appreciated because her endorsement was based on such a fine and sensitive grasp of all of its aims. And I am deeply grateful to Holly Panich and Gillian Berchowitz of the Ohio University Press for their encouragement and support in allowing me a fuller realization of those aims. Going back further in time, I probably should record my indebtedness to two former colleagues occasionally cited in these pages, Masao Miyoshi and James Kavanaugh. I certainly found their work on *Wuthering Heights* more helpful to me than they will find these lucubrations of mine. Lastly, I must thank a host of students—both undergraduates and graduates—at Berkeley, Princeton, and Bread Loaf. I have tried to keep their responses in mind whenever I invoke that putative, composite reader of *Wuthering Heights* to whom I repeatedly refer here as a collective "we" or an "us." Their attraction to a text they often found baffling and frustrating, yet always alluring, convinced me long ago of the usefulness of the kind of critical anatomy that I have tried to conduct in this little book.

U.C.K.
August 1993

Chronology

Emily Brontë's life and work	*Literary and cultural events*	*Historical events*
1818 Emily Jane Brontë born 30 July, the fifth of six children to the Reverend Patrick Brontë and Maria Branwell.	Karl Marx born. Austen, *Persuasion* and *Northanger Abbey* (posthumously); Byron, *Childe Harold IV*; Keats, *Endymion*; Peacock, *Nightmare Abbey*; Scott, *Heart of Midlothian*; Mary Shelley, *Frankenstein*.	British quell Indian uprisings; American troops occupy Spanish Florida; Ross and Franklin fail in their polar expeditions.
1819 Patrick Brontë offered perpetual curacy at Haworth, but opposed by Trustees.	Mary Ann Evans ("George Eliot") born; Charles Kingsley born; Herman Melville born; Walt Whitman born; Byron, *Don Juan I and II*; Goethe, *Westöstlicher Divan*; Keats, "Ode to a Nightingale"; Scott, *Ivanhoe*; Schopenhauer, *Die Welt als Wille und Vorstellung*.	Queen Victoria born; Peterloo massacre; repressive measures in Prussia; Lord Cochrane commands Chilean navy against Spain.
1820 Brontës move to Haworth in Yorkshire, after last child, Anne, is born; Patrick confirmed by Trustees.	Friedrich Engels born; Herbert Spencer born; *London Magazine* started; Benjamin West dies; Barrett, *Battle of Marathon*; Keats, *Lamia*; Lamb, starts "Essays of Elia"; Malthus, *Principles of Political Economy*; Percy Shelley, *Prometheus Unbound and Other Poems*.	Accession of George IV; trial of Queen Caroline taken up in House of Lords; American Congress passes the "Missouri Compromise"; revolts in Spain, Naples, and Sicily; new medicinal cures of homeopathy and hydropathy; James Monroe re-elected.

1821	Mrs. Brontë dies; "mothering" taken over by her sister, Miss Elizabeth Branwell, and by her eldest daughters Maria and Elizabeth (only 7 and 6 years old).	Baudelaire born; Flaubert born; Keats dies; Mrs. Piozzi (Hester Lynch Thrale) dies; Byron, *Don Juan* III and IV; Cobbett, *Cottage Economy*; De Quincey, *Confessions of an English Opium Eater*; Goethe, *Wilhelm Meisters Wanderjahre*; Kleist, *Prinz Friedrich von Homburg*; James Mill, *Elements of Political Economy*; Percy Shelley, *Epipsychidion* and *Adonais*.	Greek uprisings against Turkey; Napoleon dies in exile; Liberia is established for the repatriation of former slaves.
1824	Maria and Elizabeth are sent to Cowan Bridge school.	George MacDonald born; Byron dies; *Westminster Review* started; Byron, *Don Juan* XV and XVI; Carlyle translates *Wilhelm Meister*; Scott, *Redgauntlet*; Taylor translates Grimm's *Fairy Tales* (illustrated by Cruikshank).	United States and England recognize the new independent Latin American nations; Egyptians join Turkey in suppressing Greek resistance; Charles X crowned in France.
1825	Maria and Elizabeth die in May and June.	T. H. Huxley born; Anna Barbauld dies; Jacques Louis David dies; Jean Paul Richter dies; Hazlitt, *The Spirit of the Age*.	John Quincy Adams becomes President; Nicholas succeeds Alexander as Czar; railroad construction between Liverpool and Manchester approved.

1826	The four surviving children – Charlotte (10), Branwell (9), Emily (8), and Anne (6) – use toy soldiers for make-believe "play" of the Young Men; Emily chooses a "grave-looking fellow called Gravey," (also called "Parry").	Barrett, *Essay on Mind*; Cooper, *The Last of the Mohicans*; Heine, *Reisebilder*; Mary Shelley, *The Last Man*; Louis I. of Bavaria makes Munich a cultural center.	Unemployed textile workers destroy power-looms in Lancashire; Jefferson and Adams die on the fiftieth anniversary of American Independence.
1827	Children now place each pet hero on an island for the "play," of *The Islanders*; Emily chooses Arran; she and Charlotte also collaborate on "secret plays" in their joint bedroom; first extant MS by Branwell.	Ludwig van Beethoven dies; William Blake dies; Wilhelm Hauff dies; Pierre Laplace dies; University of London founded; Thomas Arnold becomes Headmaster of Rugby; Keble, *Christian Year*; Manzoni, *I Promessi Sposi*; Alfred and Charles Tennyson, *Poems By Two Brothers*.	George Canning dies and the Duke of Wellington becomes Prime Minister; Anglo-French-Russian warships destroy Turkish navy in the Battle of Navarino.
1829	Creative collaboration in full swing: the islands have become four African kingdoms of the Glasstown Confederacy; though Emily (as the Genii "Emii") presides over "Parrysland," chief chroniclers are Branwell and Charlotte.	Humphry Davy dies; Jean Baptiste Lamarck dies; Balzac, *La Comédie Humaine* begun; Carlyle, "Signs of the Times."	Catholic Emancipation Act; Peel establishes Metropolitan Police; England and Austria force Russia to make peace with Turkey; Andrew Jackson becomes President.

1830	Branwell and Charlotte continue to dominate creative activities.	Christina Rossetti born; William Hazlitt dies; *Fraser's Magazine* founded; Cobbett, *Rural Rides*; Comte, *Cours de Philosophie Positive*; Tennyson, *Poems, Chiefly Lyrical*.	Accession of William IV; July revolution in France overthrows Bourbon dynasty and crowns Louis Philippe; Bolivar dies.
1831	After Charlotte's departure for Roe Head School, Emily and Anne begin their own series, the Gondal Chronicles, in which an island created by Branwell and Charlotte is peopled with new figures, notably regal heroines.	G. W. F. Hegel dies; first meeting of British Association; Poe, *Poems*; Stendhal, *Le Rouge et le Noir*.	Russian forces occupy Poland; Reform Bill debates in British Parliament; anti-slavery movement in U.S.; revolt by Nat Turner.
1832	Emily and Anne active on "Gondals"; Branwell and Charlotte, though apart, continue partnership when possible.	C. L. Dodgson ("Lewis Carroll") born; Leslie Stephen born; Jeremy Bentham dies; J. W. Goethe dies; Sir Walter Scott dies; Darwin, *Voyages of H. M. S. Adventure and Beagle*; Goethe, *Faust II*; Tennyson, *Poems*.	Reform Bill passed; cholera epidemic; Jackson re-elected President.
1833		Oxford Movement launched by Keble's sermon on "National Apostasy"; Barrett, *Prometheus Bound*; Browning, *Pauline*; Hartley Coleridge, *Poems*; Lamb, *Last Essays of Elia*.	Civil war in Spain; revolt in Cuba.

1834		William Morris born; S. T. Coleridge dies; Charles Lamb dies; Carlyle, *Sartor Resartus* concluded in *Fraser's*; Samuel Butler born.	Slavery abolished in British West Indies and South Africa.
1835	Emily goes to Roe Head School as student and Charlotte as teacher; seriously ill after three months, Emily is replaced by Anne as pupil but quickly recovers at Haworth; Branwell fails to enroll in London art school.	Samuel Clemens ("Mark Twain") born; Andersen, *Fairy Tales*; Dickens, *Sketches by Boz*; Wordsworth, *Yarrow Revisited, and Other Poems*.	Boer settlers set up colony of their own in South Africa; Americans in Texas proclaim their separation from Mexico.
1836	First extant poem by Emily ("Will the day be bright"); Charlotte sends own poems to Southey, who advises against literary career.	Dickens, *Pickwick Papers*; Emerson, *Nature*; Heine, *Die Romantische Schule*; Meyerbeer, *Les Huguenots*; Newman, Keble, Froude, etc., *Lyra Apostolica*.	Discontent with Austrian rule in Hungary; Zulu massacre of Boers; Texan independence; Van Buren elected President.
1837	Twenty extant poems by Emily; Branwell's efforts to get noticed by Wordsworth are as unsuccessful as his letters to *Blackwood's*; Charlotte teaches; Anne studies.	Charles Algernon Swinburne born; Giacomo Leopardi dies; Alexander Pushkin dies; Carlyle, *The French Revolution*; Sara Coleridge, *Phantasmion*; Dickens, *Oliver Twist*; Thackeray, *Yellowplush Papers* (in *Fraser's*).	Accession of Queen Victoria; rebellion in Upper Canada is quelled.
1838	Twenty more poems by Emily, who returns to Haworth after a short stint as a teacher in Halifax.	Barrett, *The Seraphim*; Dickens, *Nicholas Nickleby*.	The *People's Charter* published; Cherokee Indians persecuted and Mormons exiled in United States.

1839	As governess, Anne is only steady worker; Charlotte leaves her own job as governess, Branwell gives up his artist's studio, Emily decides not to return to Halifax.	Walter Pater born; Carlyle, *Chartism*; *Shelley's Poetical Works* edited by Mary Shelley; Stendhal, *Chartreuse de Parme*; Thackeray, *Catherine* (in *Fraser's*).	Chartist agitations spread to all of England; French military expedition in Mexico and British interventions in China and Afghanistan.
1840	Branwell dismissed as tutor in a region he valued for its literary associations with De Quincey; he meets Hartley Coleridge, but receives no encouragement. Charlotte, who has written fiction about a brother and sister, sends own prose to Hartley Coleridge.	Thomas Hardy born; Emile Zola born; Fanny Burney dies; Hartley Coleridge edits Jacobean dramas; De Quincey finishes *Recollections of the Lake Poets*; Oxford Movement collects sermons in *Tracts for the Times*; Poe, *Tales of the Grotesque*.	Marriage of Queen Victoria to Prince Albert; election of Harrison ends forty years of Democrat rule in United States; Morse patents telegraph; political upheavals in Latin America.
1841	Branwell obtains position as railway clerk; plan for the three sisters to start their own school is abandoned in favor of a stay in Brussels for Charlotte and Emily.	*Punch, or The London Charivari* started; Mikhail Lermontov dies; Browning, *Pippa Passes*; Carlyle, *On Heroes, Hero-Worship, and the Heroic in History*; Emerson, *Essays: First Series*.	Corn Law debates; Tyler assumes presidency after Harrison's death; Hong Kong ceded to Britain; first Canadian Parliament convened; postage stamps.
1842	Escorted by their father, Emily and Charlotte settle in Brussels (Feb.) to study French and German. Summoned back (Nov.) by news of Aunt's abrupt death, they find Branwell home, ill and jobless.	William James born; Thomas Arnold dies; Stendhal (M-H. Beyle) dies; copyright terms extended; Dickens, *American Notes*; Tennyson, *Poems*.	Rejection of a second People's Charter results in labor strikes and the reinstatement of Wellington as commander; Afghanistan looted after British conquest.

1843	Charlotte returns to Brussels as a teacher; Branwell becomes tutor at home where Anne works as governess; Emily manages home at Haworth, as father's eyesight fails.	Henry James born; Robert Southey dies; Wordsworth becomes Poet Laureate; Borrow, *Bible in Spain*; Carlyle, *Past and Present*; Dickens, *A Christmas Carol*; Hood, *Song of the Shirt*; Ruskin, *Modern Painters* I.	Mounting social unrest: Irish opposition to legislative union with England; Hungarian opposition to Austrian rule; anti-Corn Law movement gathers strength.
1844	Emily copies poetry into two books, "Gondal Poems" and "E.J.B.," also adding new verses. Charlotte returns; fails in starting a school at parsonage and in hearing from her Brussels "master."	G. M. Hopkins born; A. B. Thorvaldsen dies; Chambers, *Vestiges of Creation*; Disraeli, *Coningsby*; Dumas, *Les Trois Mousquetaires*, *Le Comte du Monte Cristo*; Thackeray, *Barry Lyndon* (in *Fraser's*).	Polk elected President; Morse sends first telegraph message; Gold Rush in Australia.
1845	Emily resumes "Gondals" with Anne, who has decided not to rejoin Branwell at their place of employment; Branwell is dismissed, yearns for Mrs Robinson, tries to write novel. After Charlotte "accidentally" comes upon Emily's poems, she persuades sisters to publish their verses in a joint volume and to consider a similar venture in prose fiction.	Thomas Hood dies; Barrett meets Browning; Oxford Movement in crisis when Newman joins Roman Catholic church; Browning, *Dramatic Romances and Lyrics*; Disraeli, *Sybil*; Engels, *Condition of the Working Class*; Fuller, *Woman in the Nineteenth Century*; Mérimée, *Carmen*; Poe, *The Raven*.	Irish famine; annexation of Texas leads to preparations for war between Mexico and United States; Sir John Franklin sails on ill-fated Arctic expedition.

| 1846 | The "Bell brothers" pay Aylott and Jones over £40 to print *Poems by Currer, Ellis, and Acton Bell* (May); the publishers are uninterested in three stories in progress, *Wuthering Heights*, *Agnes Grey*, and *The Professor* (finished by July?). Poor reception of her work leads Charlotte to consider a longer book (August); Branwell collapses upon definitive separation from Mrs Robinson, now widowed; Mr Brontë's eyesight improved after surgery. | Barrett and Browning marry; Dickens begins *Dombey and Son*; Evans ("George Eliot") translates Strauss's *Life of Jesus*; Hawthorne, *Mosses from an Old Manse*; Lear, *Book of Nonsense*; Melville, *Typee*; Ruskin, *Modern Painters* II; Thackeray, *Book of Snobs*. | Lord Russell becomes Prime Minister after the Corn Laws are repealed; Polish revolt against Austrian rule; Mexican–American war. |
| 1847 | Unsold copies of *Poems* sent to Wordsworth, Tennyson, De Quincey, Hartley Coleridge (June); T. Newby accepts *Wuthering Heights* and *Agnes Grey*, but rejects *The Professor* (July); Smith, Elder willing to consider *Jane Eyre* instead of *The Professor* (Aug.); *Jane Eyre* published and well received (Oct.); *Wuthering Heights* published (Dec.). | Felix Mendelssohn dies; first fictions by Gaskell and Trollope published; Disraeli, *Tancred*; Tennyson, *The Princess*; Thackeray, *Vanity Fair* serialized (Jan. 1847–July 1848). | Foundation of the Communist League; Baron Rothschild barred from Parliament; Franklin expedition's fate discovered; Austrians occupy Ferrara; French and British blockade Buenos Aires; Americans occupy Mexico City. |

1848	January: *Examiner* review condemning author for failing to "refine" what is "coarse" sets tone for later critics of *Wuthering Heights*. July: Anne publishes *The Tenant of Wildfell Hall*. September: Branwell, nursed by Emily, dies; December 19: Emily dies. Manuscript of a second novel destroyed by her or, with other papers, by Charlotte.	"Pre-Raphaelite Brotherhood" formed; F. R. de Chateaubriand dies; Frederic Chopin dies; Crowe, *The Night Side of Nature*; Gaskell, *Mary Barton*; Marx and Engels, *Communist Manifesto*; Mill, *Principles of Political Economy*; Milnes, *Life of John Keats*; Newman, *Loss and Gain*.	Revolutions in France, Italy and Hungary spill into other countries; Chartist National Convention in London fails when Wellington summons troops; insurrection in Vienna quashed, though Emperor abdicates in favour of Francis Joseph; peace treaty between Mexico and United States results in acquisition of California, Arizona, and New Mexico.
1849	May: Anne dies. October: Charlotte's *Shirley* published.	Maria Edgeworth dies; Edgar Allan Poe dies; Dickens starts *Household Words*, serializes *David Copperfield*.	Italian independence quelled by Austria; California Gold Rush; Taylor inaugurated as President.
1850	December: Charlotte publishes a second edition of *Wuthering Heights* (printed with *Agnes Grey*) for which she revised Emily's text and, "laden down by memory," wrote both a "Biographical Notice" and an "Editor's Preface". She also prints more poems by Emily, including "Often Rebuked," apparently by Charlotte in Emily's persona.	Balzac dies; Wordsworth dies; Tennyson becomes Poet Laureate; E. Barrett Browning, *Poems*; R. Browning, *Christmas Eve and Easter Day*; Carlyle, *Latter Day Pamphlets*; Emerson, *Representative Men*; Keller, *Der Grüne Heinrich*; Kingsley, *Alton Locke*; F. W. Newman, *Phases of Faith*; Rossetti, *The Germ*; Spencer, *Social Statics*; Tennyson, *In Memoriam A. H. H.*; Wordsworth, *The Prelude*.	Fillmore succeeds Taylor; anti-slavery debates; first submarine telegraph between England and France.

The internal chronology of *Wuthering Heights*

Chapter	Lockwood/Nelly time	Catherine/Heathcliff time
4	Early December 1801: Nelly's narrative at Grange	Summer 1771: Heathcliff brought to Heights at age 7 (?); meets Hindley (14), Nelly (14), and Catherine (6)
5, 6		October 1777: Old Earnshaw dies; Hindley returns with Frances
3	Late Nov. 1801: Lockwood reads diary, dreams, leaves Heights	November 1777: Catherine/Heathcliff defy Hindley and Joseph
6	Dec. 1801: Nelly's story	Third week, Nov. 1777: Catherine detained at Grange; Heathcliff returns to Heights
7	break in story	Christmas Eve and Day, 1777: Catherine returns; Lintons visit Heights
8	story resumed	June 1778: Hareton born; late 78: Frances dies
9	story stopped	Summer 1780: Catherine tells Nelly she will marry Edgar; Heathcliff leaves; Catherine catches fever Autumn 1780: Elder Lintons are infected and die April 1783: Catherine marries Edgar
10	Late December 1801 (4 weeks after); Heathcliff visits Lockwood at Grange; Nelly resumes story on same day	September 1783: Heathcliff returns
11		December 1783: Nelly meets Hareton
12		10 January 1784: Catherine's delirium, Isabella elopes (2 a.m.)

30	Mid-January 1802: Nelly finishes her story; Lockwood decides to leave [6–7 weeks earlier in time]	October 1801: Linton Heathcliff dies; Hareton tries to please Cathy
1		Late November 1801: Heathcliff receives visit from his tenant at the Grange, a Mr Lockwood
2, 3		Early December 1801: Lockwood visits Heights a second time, stays overnight, sleeps in Catherine's bed, screams, is taken back to Grange by Heathcliff
31	Mid-January 1802:———	Mid-January 1802: Heathcliff is informed by Lockwood that his tenant is vacating the Grange
32	September 1802: Lockwood visits Grange, finds Nelly at Heights; she brings him up to date	February 1802: Nelly moves to Heights March 1802: Hareton has an accident; Cathy befriends him
33		March/April 1802: Cathy defies Heathcliff; Heathcliff's behavior changes
34	September 1802: Nelly ends her second narrative; Lockwood visits graves	May 1802: Heathcliff stops eating; Heathcliff dies 1 January 1803: projected wedding of Cathy and Hareton

Chapter 1

Entering *Wuthering Heights*

The context of 1850

On 10 December 1850 Charlotte Brontë brought out a second
edition of her sister Emily's *Wuthering Heights*. The first
edition of the novel, which had appeared exactly three years
earlier, hardly met with the success of Charlotte's own *Jane
Eyre* or even the milder approbation bestowed upon Anne
Brontë's *Agnes Grey*, which Charlotte also republished. Both
Anne and Charlotte had been able to capitalize on the
favourable reception of their first novels of 1847 by quickly
writing a second work of fiction: Anne had published *The
Tenant of Wildfell Hall* in July of 1848, and Charlotte had
followed with her historical novel *Shirley* in October of 1849.
No such second opportunity, however, was available to Emily
Brontë. She died on 19 December 1848, three months after her
brother Branwell, and five months before Anne. For
Charlotte, who survived into the 1850s, Emily's work urgently
required a fuller hearing than it had received so far.

That 1850 should have been considered by the last survivor
of the gifted Brontë children as the proper time for such a
hearing to occur carries a special poignancy. England itself,
historians agree, had survived a period of intense turmoil and
was ready, at mid-century, to leave behind Chartist upheavals
and the memories of the French Revolution that had been
newly stirred by the 1848 revolts on the Continent. Preparing
itself for the great international exhibition of 1851, with its
marvels of technological progress, the nation was intent on
forging a new identity and eager to stress stability and order.
It seems hardly coincidental, therefore, that 1850 also marked
the publication of Alfred Tennyson's own progress poem
about the formation of a stabler identity. Indeed, *In

Memoriam, A. H. H. proved so successful in capturing the
public mood that it gained Tennyson the Laureateship upon
the death of William Wordsworth. Wordsworth's own
layered reconstruction of personal growth, *The Prelude*, was
less noticed when it too appeared, posthumously, in 1850. A
shared social self seemed to have displaced Romantic
self-inquiry.

To transform the private into the communal had become,
more than ever, the order of the day. Leigh Hunt, already the
most sociable of the Romantics, made his long-dead peers
seem human and accessible in the reminiscences of his anec-
dotal *Autobiography*; Elizabeth Barrett Browning moved
from reclusiveness to the celebration of communion in her
Sonnets from the Portuguese; Francis W. Newman
scrupulously shared the recreated stages of his religious
transformation in *Phases of Faith*; Charles Kingsley attacked
class barriers in his polemical novel *Alton Locke*. Small
wonder, then, that Charlotte Brontë, who had herself moved
from the romance and first-person narrative of *Jane Eyre* to
the wider social panorama of *Shirley*, should be so eager
to break the barriers that impeded the 1850 reader from
appreciating the hermetic *Wuthering Heights*. To make her
sister's work suit the spirit of the times, Charlotte would have
to act — so she thought — as a mediator. "An interpreter
ought always to have stood," she asserted, between her sister
"and the world." She decided to become Emily's interpreter,
to familiarize readers with a self buried in the complicated,
layered structure of *Wuthering Heights*.

As far as Charlotte was concerned, the reclamation of this
buried self required, first of all, an attempt to apprise
Victorian readers of the differences among, and the inter-
relatedness of, the identities of the three collaborating sisters
who had first broken into print by using the pseudonyms of
Currer, Ellis, and Acton Bell. Their 1846 volume of collected
poems, little noticed and published at their own expense, had
been triggered by Charlotte's accidental discovery of Emily's
poems, which she deemed to be superior to her own and to
Anne's. Despite the ill success of *Poems by Currer, Ellis, and*

Acton Bell, the trio decided to get their fictions into print. Reverting back to the time when, joined by their now excluded brother Branwell, they had assiduously worked on stories, the "reunited" sisters tried out on each other the novels by which they hoped to capture a Victorian reading public. Although Charlotte's *The Professor* was rejected, a publisher (Smith and Elder) encouraged her to write a three-volume novel; *Jane Eyre* appeared before the novels by Anne and Emily, which a less efficient and responsible publisher (T. Newby) had much earlier accepted. Since both *Wuthering Heights* and Anne's *Agnes Grey* (which filled two and one volumes, respectively, in Newby's three-volume set) had been marred by typographical mistakes, Charlotte revised both books punctiliously in her 1850 re-issue. And, to remove "the obscurity attending those two names – Ellis and Acton," she also wrote a "Biographical Notice" to acquaint a new audience with the genesis of the two novels and with the personalities of their authors.

Ostensibly devoted to both of her sisters, Charlotte's "Biographical Notice of Ellis and Acton Bell" pays considerably more attention to Emily or "Ellis Bell." Whereas Anne is depicted as compliant, "quietly" producing some of "her own compositions, intimating that since Emily's had given me pleasure, I might look at hers," Emily herself is shown to resist any such intrusion into "the recesses" of her "mind and feelings," even by "those nearest and dearest to her." It is this resistance, Charlotte Brontë suggests, that somehow allowed Emily to preserve a greater originality: just as the poems she had concealed "were not common effusions, not at all like the poetry women generally write," so were the "very real powers revealed in *Wuthering Heights*" uniquely and idiosyncratically her own. Yet if, according to Charlotte, Anne lacked "the power, the fire, the originality of her sister," Emily's "unbending" preservation of her "secret" gifts also proved costly. The "import and nature" of *Wuthering Heights* were too easily "misunderstood." And the reluctance of its author to engage her audience in the way that Charlotte's Jane Eyre addresses a "dear reader" allowed some critics to assume that the book "was an earlier and ruder attempt of the same pen which had produced *Jane Eyre*," a notion that the "Biographical Notice" is designed to lay at rest.

"I *am* Heathcliff," says Catherine Earnshaw in her crucial confession to Nelly Dean in *Wuthering Heights* (ch. 9). She is attracted to him, she adds "because he's more myself than I am." Although Charlotte Brontë wants to make clear to an 1850 audience that neither she, "Currer Bell," nor "Acton Bell" *were* "Ellis Bell," she also acknowledges her special identification with Emily. That *Wuthering Heights* tantalized her much more than *Agnes Grey* is evident from her omission of Anne's first novel in the account of the "Biographical Notice." (It is significant, in this respect, that Charlotte should devote a paragraph to *The Tenant of Wildfell Hall*, for, as we shall see in the last chapter of this study, Anne's second novel, which Charlotte declares to be "morbid," itself contains a reaction to *Wuthering Heights*.)

Charlotte Brontë's "Biographical Notice," then, is shaped by a dynamic similar to that of *Wuthering Heights* itself. Just as Emily's novel simultaneously demands and qualifies the reader's identification with Heathcliff, so does Charlotte's rhetoric invite sympathy for Heathcliff's creator while also maintaining a wary distance from a sister she sees as having possibly been more herself than she was. Emily is said to lack the "worldly wisdom" to which the author of this public "Notice" presumably acquiesced. And yet Emily's very refusal to adapt herself to "the world" endows her with what are described as Heathcliffian energies: "a secret power and fire that might have informed the brain and kindled the veins of a hero." Just as Heathcliff mesmerizes the characters who come under his spell – old Earnshaw, Catherine, Isabella, Hareton, Lockwood – so does Charlotte find it difficult to dissociate herself from her sister's power and fire. As inflexible as a Heathcliff who resists domestication, Emily thus needs to be made more palatable to the 1850 reader who can value the work of "Currer," but not "Ellis," "Bell."

Therefore, to re-edit Emily's book and to add the

"Biographical Notice" still seemed insufficient to Charlotte Brontë. The novel itself had to be reclaimed and interpreted by her. To complete her act of mediation Charlotte attached still another document to the 1850 re-issue of *Wuthering Heights*: the critical essay she called "Editor's Preface to the New Edition of *Wuthering Heights*." Since that extraordinary essay was designed to act as the outer layer of the many we traverse as we move through the narrative of *Wuthering Heights*, we must consider it as our point of entry into the novel.

Charlotte Brontë's 1850 "Editor's Preface"

Charlotte Brontë's decision to add her "Editor's Preface" to *Wuthering Heights* gave her a share in her dead sister's novel. Charlotte had twice rejected the idea of writing a preface for her own *Shirley* during the previous year; she felt no compunction whatsoever to provide one for the re-issued *Agnes Grey*. And she was more than aware that Emily Brontë, whose reclusiveness she repeatedly stressed in the "Biographical Notice," would hardly have wanted to communicate in this fashion with her own readers. Still, since Emily held for Charlotte the status of a shared former self, her survivor could cling to the notion that Emily might have developed to become as other-directed as Charlotte herself had become: "Had she but lived, her mind would itself have grown like a strong tree, loftier, straighter, wider-spreading, and its matured fruits would have attained a mellower ripeness and sunnier bloom; but on that mind time and experience alone could work: to the influence of other intellects, it was not amenable."

Although Emily's "mind" had ceased to operate, *Wuthering Heights* – the chief product of that mind – might benefit, Charlotte seems to imply, from the time and experience of a caring sister-editor. The "Editor's Preface" thus is designed to smooth down the novel Charlotte likens to a "granite block." Just as, at the end of *Wuthering Heights*, the tombstone of Edgar Linton is depicted as "harmonized by the turf, and moss creeping up its foot" (ch. 34), so does the

"Editor's Preface" conclude by metaphorically softening Emily's "crag"-like handiwork. The form – "half statue, half rock" – which Emily has left behind is now clothed in "moorland moss" and toned down with a "colouring" of "mellow grey." If, as Charlotte contends, her sister's mind steadily resisted the influence of other intellects, the stark form that Emily "moulded" can at least become more "amenable" through the imagistic overlay provided by a mellower and riper fellow-novelist. Still, the "Editor's Preface" also seems to acknowledge that ripeness is *not* all, that there is something powerfully inviolable in the "unredeemed" Heathcliffian energies of *Wuthering Heights*. Mediation may be necessary, as necessary as the fragmentation of the sororal and fraternal selves on which the structure of *Wuthering Heights* rests. But if this fragmentation – which now holds a special significance for Charlotte Brontë – is inevitable, there is also something hypnotically compelling in the resistance to change by a mind eager to burrow back to a child-like sense of an unsundered unity between self and other.

While conceding the importance of the "matured" outlook that would have made *Wuthering Heights* more acceptable to a civilized reader, Charlotte Brontë seems to allow that the book's "power" comes precisely from its author's refusal to yield to what civilization defines as maturation or growth. Emily's imagination has fashioned a construct described as "rustic," "rude," "simple," "homely," and "wild." And yet that rusticity remains "more original" and "more truthful" because more in touch with something elemental than any "wider" or "more comprehensive" treatment by a writer better educated than a "homebred girl." By valuing the primal energies her sister had tapped, Charlotte appears to recognize that the book depicted the same sort of return to an imaginative fountainhead also found in the more successful literary productions of 1850. Dickens, for example, had traced back to the orphaned David Copperfield the emotional powers of childhood and adolescence which were the mainspring of his adult creativity. And Tennyson, in the above-mentioned *In Memoriam A. H. H.*, animated a "dead self" bonded to his dead friend Arthur Hallam in order to be able to "rise on stepping stones . . . to higher things."

Charlotte Brontë read Tennyson's poem around the time she was editing both *Wuthering Heights* and Emily's verses, many of which had been previously unprinted. As eager as Tennyson to "find in loss a gain," she nonetheless regarded *In Memoriam* as being too artificial in its expression of that loss. Given the extent of her identification with the "truthful" Emily, it seems significant that Charlotte should have questioned the "stamp of truth" of *In Memoriam*. She maintained that "if Arthur Hallam had been somewhat nearer Alfred Tennyson – his brother instead of his friend – I should have distrusted this rhymed, and measured, and printed monument of grief" (27 August 1850, letter to Elizabeth Gaskell). Tennyson, Charlotte here implies, had captured a huge audience for himself by his ability to cast his grief for a brother-poet into "measured" verse; Emily, on the other hand, whose *Wuthering Heights* treats the immoderate grief of a brother-self sundered from its female complement, had died unknown and unacknowledged. She deserved a "monument" herself. Charlotte would obtain that audience for the dead genius she had appropriated as her own *alter ego*.

But in trying to secure for Emily the audience she had herself found through *Jane Eyre* and *Shirley*, Charlotte Brontë also had to confront – and indirectly try to vindicate – the "measured" compromises through which she had obtained the status of a popular novelist. In her efforts to woo the reader of 1850 into accepting *Wuthering Heights* as a major literary landmark, she was compelled to review what she regarded as her sister's total intransigence towards the tastes and expectations of such a reader. As Carl Woodring first noted in a 1957 essay ("The Narrators of *Wuthering Heights*"), Emily may actually have facilitated an opposition to her own fable by attributing to her first and "outer" narrator, young Lockwood, the puzzled responses she anticipated her book might well receive from an average mid-Victorian male reader. As Woodring puts it: "If [Lockwood] seems inane, he suffers from the inanity his author attributes to the average London reader into whose hands her book will fall." In her "Editor's Preface," where she casts herself as her sister's prime reader — "the auditor of her work when read in manuscript" — Charlotte professes to have anticipated some of the resistance which an ordinary reader of the printed book might well feel towards its depiction of human characters and events even more "alien" than its remote setting. Would not such an audience be disposed to reject what Charlotte herself found too disturbing when she had "shuddered under the grinding influence of natures so relentless and implacable, of spirits so lost and fallen"? Yet Emily, according to Charlotte's account, had shrugged off such a response: "if it was complained that the mere hearing of certain vivid and fearful scenes banished sleep by night, and disturbed mental peace by day, Ellis Bell would wonder what was meant, and suspect the complainant of affectation."

What were those "vivid and fearful scenes" that professedly unsettled Charlotte Brontë at the time of the composition of *Wuthering Heights*? Given her own rendition of haunting dreams, premonitions and eerie voices in *Jane Eyre*, she seems to have in mind more than the ghost which Lockwood repels in his dream in chapter 3 or the tortures which Heathcliff inflicts on others as well as on himself. Her sister appears to have touched on personal elements which Charlotte would have preferred her to avoid. (We shall return to Charlotte's own concealments in both "The Editor's Preface" and the "Biographical Notice" after we have delved into the novel and examined some of the taboos it possibly transgressed.) At any rate, Charlotte's ambivalent mixture of revulsion and fascination leads her to describe *Wuthering Heights* in terms similar to those which an older Mary Shelley used to describe the "very hideous" story she had written while still "a young girl." Hindsight is needed to offset the "horror" that "broods" over *Wuthering Heights*, which Charlotte describes as if it were indeed Shelley's *Frankenstein*: a "storm-heated and electrical atmosphere," in which "we seem at times to breathe lightning," demands a guide who can "point to those spots where clouded daylight and the eclipsed sun still attest their existence." The irrational night-side of nature Emily Brontë so forcefully depicted thus somehow requires the sunlight of reason as its complement.

Charlotte's "Preface" makes clear that she expects to provide such a complement by pointing out those lighter "spots" which might endear *Wuthering Heights* to the average reader. Her special pleading, however well-intentioned, seems amiss. Shying away from the "unredeemed" Heathcliff even more than Mary Shelley, in her own 1831 Preface to *Frankenstein*, shied away from her own "hideous progeny," the Monster, Charlotte uneasily tries to redress her sister's presumed monstrosities by looking for characters whose dubious social virtues she can emphasize: "For a specimen of true benevolence and fidelity, look at the character of Nelly Dean; for an example of constancy and tenderness, remark that of Edgar Linton." Such instructions may be designed to help a certain kind of mid-Victorian reader overcome objections to what at first glance "must appear a rude and strange production." Still, by reducing characters to near-allegorical abstractions ("a dry and saturnine humour in the delineation of old Joseph, and some glimpses of grace and gaiety" in that of "the younger Catherine"), Charlotte Brontë makes her sister's book appear rather static and mechanical. She thus actually endorses the notion of a rudimentary "production" she is so eager to discredit.

Curiously enough, the starting and the concluding sentences of the "Editor's Preface" mimic the phrasing employed by Lockwood in his own opening and closing of the book. Both Lockwood and Charlotte Brontë begin with the words "I have just" to describe their entry into an unfamiliar terrain which, as each notes, is far removed from urban civilization. Both Lockwood and Charlotte Brontë end their respective accounts by trying to soften their exit from this elementary world. Although their reasons for wanting to subdue the harshness they leave behind are very different, both stress the evidence of a more benign growth. Thus, the tombstones Lockwood inspects are surrounded by "turf" and creeping "moss"; and Lockwood himself, watching "the moths fluttering among the heath and hare-bells" and listening to the "soft wind breathing through the grass," wonders "how any one could ever imagine unquiet slumbers in that quiet earth" (ch. 34). The narrator of the 1850 "Editor's Preface" introduces a similar note of quietism. Trying to erase the imprint left by the "terrible and goblin-like" features of the half-finished "statue" hewed by the "chisel" of an Emily metaphorically transformed into a male sculptor, this artist paints a pastoral canvas. Resorting to Lockwood's lyricism, the painter wants the "swart" and "sinister" statue to become less dramatic, "almost beautiful, for its colouring is of mellow grey, and moorland grass clothes it; and heath with its blooming bells and balmy fragrance, grows faithfully close to the giant's foot." A mourner seems to have deposited Lockwood's bell-flowers on an entombed sister's novel. Signing herself "CURRER BELL" at the foot of the last sentence, Charlotte Brontë tries to remain as "faithfully close" as possible to her initial awe of the novel she treats as a Gothic colossus. Unlike Lockwood, who winds up denying the power that originally attracted him to the Heights, she merely wants to bring that power into closer contact with the quotidian motions of life.

The reader and Mr. Lockwood

Charlotte Brontë's adoption of Lockwood's rhetoric for her entry and exit in "The Editor's Preface," whether conscious or not, betokens her understanding of the role which Emily had assigned to this figure in the scheme of *Wuthering Heights*. Lockwood acts as the reader's prime agent. His initial willingness to partake of a reality peopled by characters totally alien to his previous experience becomes congruous with that of any reader who ventures into the book. We follow Lockwood in the opening paragraphs as he eagerly presses against the "barrier" that Heathcliff (and a part of Emily Brontë herself) would prefer to keep chained. But

Lockwood will soon be tested. The man so eager to penetrate "Mr. Heathcliff's dwelling" in chapter 1 will find it increasingly difficult to gain true access to its interior. As he notes on first crossing its threshold, the house called "Wuthering Heights" has narrow windows, extra-thick walls, and "corners defended with large jutting stones" (ch. 1). As soon as he tries to familiarize himself − and us − with the structure's content, Lockwood meets with difficulties that cause him to become highly defensive. Although his curiosity and avowed empathy lead him to seek out a better informant in Nelly Dean, who replaces him as chief narrator in chapter 4, he gradually loses interest in the inhabitants of the Heights.

Lockwood thus anticipates the responses of most of the earlier readers of the book, as Emily Brontë undoubtedly expected him to do. For through her creation of this well-meaning but imperfect medium, she could test her putative audience and determine their fitness as trespassers into the verbal structure that bears the name of the house into which Lockwood has stumbled. Although both he and the reader are jointly put on probation, we must press beyond him. Whereas he too readily withdraws his professed "sympathy" for the inmates of the Heights, we are allowed to expand our own identification with the various characters.

Emily Brontë's skillful impersonation of Lockwood as the first "I" we meet in her novel challenges Charlotte's claims, in the "Editor's Preface," about the unsophisticated nature of the "homebred country girl" who, "as a native and nursling of the moors," markedly differed from "a lady or gentleman accustomed to what is called 'the world'." For Lockwood's voice, which dominates the narrative until displaced by that of Nelly Dean, is that of an urban young gentleman whose sophistication and "worldliness" prove to be inadequate. His subordination to Nelly is significant in this respect. Although she is someone who has been "living among the hills and seeing one set of faces," the house-keeper is hardly the provincial he makes her out to be; as Nelly points out to Lockwood, "I have read more than you would fancy" (ch. 7). His condescension towards "people in these regions" is misplaced.

From the very start, Lockwood seems uncomfortable not just about the appropriateness of his responses to what he observes in a reality so different from his own, but also about the language in which he couches such responses. His first exchange with Heathcliff, which he reproduces in the opening paragraphs, is marked by a retrospective insecurity that finds release through ironic inflections. What are we to make of Lockwood's attitudes towards the Heathcliff we first behold through his eyes? Is he genuinely drawn to a man who so rudely dispenses with the formalities of polite intercourse, or is he trying to salvage his ruffled feelings by trying to laugh both at Heathcliff and himself? Can these possibilities be simultaneously entertained? Emily Brontë entangles us at the outset by forcing us to participate in Lockwood's confused and ambivalent flounderings:

1801 − I have just returned from a visit to my landlord − the solitary neighbour that I shall be troubled with. This is certainly a beautiful country! In all of England, I do not believe that I could have fixed on a situation so completely removed from the stir of society. A perfect misanthropist's heaven − and Mr. Heathcliff and I are such a suitable pair to divide the desolation between us. A capital fellow! He little imagined how my heart warmed towards him when I beheld his black eyes withdraw so suspiciously under their brows, as I rode up, and when his fingers sheltered themselves, with a jealous resolution, still further in his waistcoat, as I announced my name.

"Mr. Heathcliff?" I said.

A nod was the answer.

"Mr. Lockwood, your new tenant, sir. I do myself the honour of calling as soon as possible after my arrival, to express the hope that I have not inconvenienced you by my perseverance in soliciting the occupation of Thrushcross Grange: I heard, yesterday, you had had some thoughts − "

"Thrushcross Grange is my own, sir," he interrupted, wincing, "I should not allow any one to inconvenience me, if I could hinder it − walk in!"

The "walk in," was uttered with closed teeth and expressed the sentiment, "Go to the Deuce!". Even the gate over which he leant manifested no sympathizing movement to the words, and I think the circumstance determined me to accept the invitation: I felt interested in a man who seemed more exaggeratedly reserved than myself.

(ch. 1)

A close inspection of Brontë's brilliant opening reveals a series of frictions which Lockwood's language vainly tries to avoid. It is not just that Lockwood's polite diction fails to bring about the conversation he has expected between himself and Heathcliff, but it becomes equally apparent that the "sympathizing movement" that he wants to convey through the words he uses in his initial description may be equally forced. Lockwood does not announce his own name, as he claims to do, at the end of the first paragraph. Instead, he asks, "Mr. Heathcliff?," only to receive no verbal reply. Heathcliff's silent nod suggests his hostility to language such as Lockwood will now use in addressing his "landlord." But Heathcliff's silence also mocks the elaborateness of the first paragraph's attempt to situate the speaker in a world so "removed from the stir of society" that it calls into question his social phraseology. His two exclamatory outbursts – "This is certainly a beautiful country!" "A capital fellow!" – seem suspect, all the more so when we discover that they have been made after the rebuffs poor Lockwood suffers in the first chapter. Are they, therefore, to be read with an ironic or sarcastic intonation? And how are we to take the seemingly innocuous phrase "I shall be troubled with" in the very first sentence? Does Lockwood anticipate, on the basis of this first visit, trouble from the "solitary neighbour" he professes to value for that very solitariness? If Lockwood were *not* to trouble himself with one potentially troublesome to his equipoise he could indeed be said to prize solitude. As it is, however, and as the remainder of the first chapter further illustrates, Lockwood's avowed desire for country seclusion seems something of a pose. This chatty young man, we soon come to realize, finds it very difficult to remain alone.

Lockwood's interest in one who seems "more exaggerated-ly reserved than myself" thus casts into doubt the nature and extent of his own reserve. Can a genuine misanthropist really join another as a "suitable pair"? A true hater of humanity, Fielding's Man on the Hill, for example, in *Tom Jones*, would hardly want someone to share his isolation. Such a man's "heart" would no more be "warmed" towards one who refuses to shake his hand than it would welcome a gregarious tenant who insists on pushing his way past the hindrances of a "perfect misanthropist's heaven." Perhaps Lockwood's heart is "warmed" by something other than fellow-feeling. Rejection, after all, can also make one heated. Attuned to contradiction, the alert Lockwood notices that the invitation he has extracted from Heathcliff may actually imply its opposite. It is the mode of delivery that matters: a "walk in" that is uttered through closed teeth may indeed express "the sentiment, 'Go to the Deuce!'" Lockwood's own mode of delivery also reveals, for all its conventional phrasing, an emphasis different from that which lies on the surface. If he feels an interest in what the reserved Heathcliff may conceal, so does the reader become interested in what may lie underneath Lockwood's own polite formulations. Is this would-be solitary attracted to the asocial nature of the "handsome" and "rather morose" Heathcliff because he feels himself at odds with the culture that has stamped him? Lockwood's unsuspected capacity for savagery when he, too, will resist the advances of an invader in chapter 3 suggests that his civilized veneer, expressed through his language, hides something more anarchic and passionate. Not only Catherine Earnshaw, with whose defiant behavior he will identify in the first of his two dreams, but Lockwood himself seems strongly drawn to Heathcliff as an *alter ego* more capable of being what he would like to be.

"The sympathetic chord" that Lockwood at first will claim as binding him to Heathcliff may stem, as he notes, from an act of projection: "I bestow my own attributes over-liberally on him" (ch. 1). But the reverse seems just as possible. Lockwood extracts from Heathcliff attributes he has been led to shed or subdue in the course of his own socialization as an educated young gentleman. His identification with Heathcliff is hardly as full as that of Catherine who, despite her own social development from primitive freedom to lady-like constraints, cannot cut off the Heathcliff-self to which she is bound. Still, though less of a sharer, Lockwood at least seems capable of understanding the bond which Catherine and

Heathcliff so strongly felt as children. It is no coincidence that Catherine, eager to return to Heathcliff, should later materialize in Lockwood's dream. He is, after all, sleeping in the "oak case," that curious panelled "structure," that was once her bed; and he has been reading the rebellious diary she wrote when she and the boy Heathcliff were still unsundered (ch. 3).

There is indeed something boyish about Lockwood for all his studied efforts at adult courtesy. The "inanity" Woodring and other readers have accused Lockwood of displaying is nowhere more in evidence than in his childish efforts to revenge himself on "the canine mother" who has rebuffed his advances even more than Heathcliff (ch. 1). Finding his efforts to caress "madam" rewarded with a wolfish snarl and "white teeth watering for a snatch" at his legs, Lockwood tries to get even with the dog he finally calls a "ruffianly bitch" by secretly "winking and making faces" at her and two of her companions. The irritation he produces brings on an attack by an entire pack of "four-footed fiends" both in chapter 1, and, once again, in chapter 2, when the servant Joseph loosens Gnasher and Wolf on a Lockwood who now retorts, even more incongruously, "with several incoherent threats of retaliation that, in their infinite depth of virulency" – and also in their impotence – "smacked of King Lear" at the height of his humiliation (ch. 3).

Such behavior, though wonderfully ludicrous, suggests why Lockwood is originally so strongly drawn to the Heights. He is fascinated by a house in which Heathcliff's anti-social behavior is shared by the other inhabitants, both human and canine. Only the servant Zillah, who calls the young visitor a "poor lad" (ch. 2) and offers him the dubious shelter of the dead Catherine's bed, and "a brindled, grey cat" (ch. 3), who salutes and joins him after his nightmare, prove to be mildly sociable. (Earlier, in an essay she wrote for her French master in Brussels on "Le Chat," Emily Brontë deemed feline self-reliance to be superior to the hypocrisy of human professions of selflessness.) Although Lockwood becomes the butt of the primitive ways he half-celebrates and half-mocks, his

uncertainty about his place in the world from which he comes
contributes to his interest in "a situation so completely
removed from the stir of society." Lockwood painfully
remembers what "my dear mother used to say" when she
predicted that "I should never have a comfortable home"
(ch. 1) – which, in modern parlance, translates to something
like, "this boy will never amount to anything."

The little vignette Lockwood provides of his most recent
mishap before his arrival in the country confirms his social
maladroitness. Having flirted with a "real goddess" of a
young lady at a coastal spa, Lockwood stole away as soon as
he detected the slightest reciprocation of his feelings: "And
what did I do? I confess it with shame – shrunk icily into
myself, like a snail . . . till, finally, the poor innocent was led
to doubt her own senses, and overwhelmed with confusion at
her supposed mistake, persuaded her mamma to decamp"
(ch. 1). In a novel abounding in immature lovers,
Lockwood's uneasy and comical amphibian position between
adolescence and sexual maturity proves to be as significant an
avenue for the book's central conflicts as does his equally
uneasy hovering between naturalness and artifice. Lockwood
will evade what might easily have unfolded for him at the
Heights. He soon prefers the relative safety of Thrushcross
Grange, where he delegates to Nelly Dean an authority similar
to that which he attributes to "my dear mother" by allowing
her to take on the responsibilities of narration.

But even Nelly's closer, eye-witness account of events,
marked by a defensiveness that often seems more pronounced
than Lockwood's own, proves to be unreliable, as so many
critics have noted. Nelly's decided stake in events that affect
her and which she tries to shape make her far more biased
than the casually involved Lockwood. Whereas she tries to
convert her listeners to her own point of view, Lockwood is
content to take us across the threshold of a structure we are
then free to scrutinize more thoroughly on our own.
Lockwood's chief asset for the reader, therefore, remains his
initial receptivity. Relatively free from prejudices, his mind is
still closer to that unencumbered *tabula rasa* which John

Locke attributed to the very young (Locke's "wood"?). He thus is better suited as a respondent to characters and events than an older and more firmly entrenched member of a patriarchal society might have been. Indeed, as James H. Kavanagh has argued, Nelly Dean's identification with "the patriarchal power of the Law and Word" make her as much of an actor in the novel's power-struggles as Heathcliff himself (*Emily Brontë*, Oxford and New York, 1985). Lockwood, on the other hand, by his very inactivity, helps to activate the reader. As the historian of the two families of the Heights and Grange, Nelly will push her own version of the past. As one who finds no time to elicit "a short history of the place from the surly owner," the entering Lockwood barely has time to note the date "1500" and the name "Hareton Earnshaw." The reader, not he, will have to piece together what lurks beyond the "family sitting-room" into which Lockwood has stumbled.

Though Lockwood will recoil once more, snail-like, into himself, the peripheral position he maintains after chapter 3 seems appropriate. His earlier openness to Heathcliff, to the first Catherine as a girl and to the second Catherine as a young woman, is brief and guarded. But that openness nonetheless makes him a prime link between the reader and Emily Brontë. Even his marked insecurities become a virtue of sorts. Lockwood's own "situation" is shown to be decidedly marginal: he is male, though unmasculine; he is grown up, and yet quite childish; he is urbane and well-educated, but fascinated by anti-social and non-verbal behavior. Intelligent, but at the same time undeniably silly, this blundering young man is still relatively free from the formulations by which a late eighteenth-century or early nineteenth-century orthodoxy defined the stability of its members. His reliance on the language by which his culture stabilized meaning has become problematic, as the "troubled" youth seems increasingly to recognize. For his linguistic equipment becomes especially inadequate when he must face, not just a dubious *alter ego* in Heathcliff, but also a missing female complement such as the one Heathcliff so intensely desires.

Lockwood, language, and the feminine

Lockwood's circumlocutions, his Latinisms, and his fondness for ready-made phrases give his speech an artificiality that contravenes what Wordsworth had called, around the same time that Brontë sets her story, "the language really spoken by men" (1800 Preface to *Lyrical Ballads*). By the end of chapter 1 Lockwood has at last succeeded in drawing Heathcliff into the verbal exchange that seemed so unlikely at the outset. He smugly notes that his host has "relaxed a little, in the laconic style of chipping off his pronouns and auxiliary words," as soon as he introduced a more conventional "discourse on the advantages and disadvantages of my present place of retirement" (ch. 1). Professing himself "encouraged" by such polite discourse, Lockwood immediately volunteers a second visit to the Heights, only to be rebuffed once again: "He evidently wished no repetition of my intrusion. I shall go, notwithstanding. It is astonishing how sociable I feel myself compared with him" (ch. 1). The concluding remark suggests that Lockwood's pushiness may have little to do with his relishing still another predictable chit-chat about rural retirement. Quite to the contrary, he seems to have welcomed Heathcliff's gruffness: Lockwood's self-aggrandizing profession that, had he been bitten by the dog Juno, he "would have set my signet on the biter," elicited a grin from his host. Aware of his foolishness, the youth who refers to pots and pans as "culinary utensils," who calls a front entrance "the penetralium," who prefers "canine mother" to "bitch," who feels compelled to furnish a pedantic definition of the "significant provincial adjective" of "Wuthering," seems, by his very linguistic self-consciousness, to welcome the relief of chipped-off pronouns and auxiliary words. And, indeed, by chapter 3 Lockwood will endorse the child Catherine's defiance of Joseph's fraudulent language.

But when, in the second chapter, Lockwood returns to the Heights, he finds, instead of the "maister" with whom he expected to have a drink, "nobbut t' missis," as Joseph informs him. And his need to account for this unsuspected female presence now leads Lockwood into a series of embarrassing mental confusions and verbal entanglements. In quick succession, he manages to offend each of the three people he tries to flatter. He first upsets Cathy, whose "cool, regardless manner" seems to unnerve him far more than Heathcliff's previous rudeness, when he unintentionally calls attention to her subordinate status. And he then agitates Heathcliff and Hareton when he misconstrues the nature of their relation to "Mrs. Heathcliff." In each case, his strained efforts at gallantry recoil on him and contribute to his uneasiness about the role of a worldly young man that he has dubiously tried to assume.

Seeing "something like cats on a cushion," Lockwood commits his first slip. Trying to endear himself to the aloof young woman who has repelled his small-talk about Juno and her pups, he assumes that she prefers kittens, "Ah, your favourites are among these!" Her renewed scorn makes him see that the furry "favourites" were merely a "heap of dead rabbits" (ch. 2). His next compliment only aggravates the situation. When he extravagantly vows that Cathy is "the proper person to ask" him to stay for tea, he pains her by reminding her of her powerlessness. The gentlewoman whom Lockwood will continue to mistake as mistress of the house now frowns and pouts, her "red under-lip pushed out, ready to cry" (ch. 2).

Lockwood's subsequent mistakes about the relations among the inhabitants of the Heights will center, significantly enough, on this attractive young female with the "red under-lip." His own relation to the opposite sex is now called into question. Lockwood repeatedly fails to see that he is hardly expected to perform the role of flattering courtier by the woman whose manner he finds more and more "embarrassing and disagreeable." Instead of recognizing Cathy as a fellow-outsider, someone whose powerlessness resembles his own and whose main sustenance, like his, comes from the books she so avidly reads, Lockwood persists in magnifying her status, elevating as head of the household one who has actually been placed below the servants. When Lockwood also endows her with erotic powers, this fictive transformation proves to be troublesome, even for him. The young man who could not sustain his earlier flirtation with the "real goddess" he met at the sea-shore is not prepared to pay homage to still another potential threat. He therefore prefers to convert Cathy into the wife of either one of the two virile figures who now join them – Heathcliff and Hareton, whose roughness Lockwood again remarks, though he now also recognizes a superiority in "bearing."

Unwilling to allow that the "admirable" female "form" before him – one "apparently scarcely past girlhood" – might be unmarried (a relative of Heathcliff's, or possibly even his daughter), Lockwood first assigns her the position of Heathcliff's wife, and then, upon discovering, that she is his host's daughter-in-law, marries her off to Hareton, whom he wrongly assumes to be Heathcliff's son. In each case, Lockwood's error is exacerbated by the bombastic phrasing on which he relies. And in each case, the error also provokes a passionate outburst from two men whose capacity to feel is so much more intense than Lockwood's own. Lockwood's self-esteem – indeed, his sense of his own masculinity – is thus severely shaken. Instead of welcoming Cathy as one who is as much in conflict with authority as he is and instead of sensing that this defiant female is capable of an ironic playfulness quite similar to his own, Lockwood falls back on the stereotypes of his culture. He is shocked to see Heathcliff "savagely" reprimand the young woman in his presence. Yet afraid of either standing up to Heathcliff or questioning such uncivilized behavior, Lockwood prefers to pretend that his surroundings are perfectly idyllic. He holds it his "duty" to "dispel" all vestiges of "ill-tempered" conduct by lamely falling back on some ready-made phrases about pastoral contentment.

Whether or not Lockwood thinks that he can get away with such palpable insincerities remains unclear, but he little anticipates how – and why – his words will be thrown back at him by an aroused Heathcliff. Politeness over balanced tea-cups will not work under these circumstances:

"It is strange," I began in the interval of swallowing one cup of tea and receiving another, "it is strange how custom can mould our tastes and ideas; many could not imagine the existence of happiness in a life of such complete exile from the world as you spend, Mr. Heathcliff; yet, I'll venture to say, that, surrounded by your family, and with your amiable lady as the presiding genius of your home and heart − "

"My amiable lady!" he interrupted, with an almost diabolical sneer on his face. "Where is she − my amiable lady?"

"Mrs. Heathcliff, your wife, I mean."

"Well, yes − Oh! you would intimate that her spirit has taken the post of ministering angel, and guards the fortunes of Wuthering Heights, even when her body is gone. Is that it?"

Perceiving my blunder, I attempted to correct it. I might have seen there was too great a disparity between the ages of the parties to make it likely that they were man and wife.   (ch. 2)

By turning Lockwood's "presiding genius of your home and heart" into the equally trite "post of ministering angel," Heathcliff mocks a language depleted of all vitality through its over-use. But Heathcliff's allusion to a "spirit" also suggests that more than Lockwood's linguistic blunders are at stake here. For in this exchange Emily Brontë first introduces a love relation that ultimately cannot be rendered through conventional language. The triple repetition of "amiable lady" conveys the loss of someone who, as far as Heathcliff is concerned, ceased to be "amiable" as soon as she opted to become a "lady." "Where is she?," Heathcliff asks rhetorically, anticipating his plaintive cry, a chapter later, "Oh! my heart's darling, hear me *this* time − Catherine, at last!" (ch. 3). Where, indeed, is the "she" that was once at one with Heathcliff? Can she be recaptured? The dead Catherine is as elusive as the ghost-child in Wordsworth's poem "Lucy Gray." And language itself, for Emily Brontë as much as for a Romantic poet such as Wordsworth, is symptomatic of a fall from some pre-linguistic and unselfconscious unity. Lockwood's verbal self-consciousness only alerts us to our entry into a world in which a Fall has already taken place. He − and we − are here allowed our first glimpse of that Fall's aftermath.

When Heathcliff derisively refers to the "spirit" of a

disembodied wife who guards the fortunes of the Heights, he is, of course, no longer referring to the dead Catherine but rather to his former wife Isabella. And yet the being he loves is herself a "spirit," even if that word remains questionable, as questionable as the term "ghosts," applied to both Heathcliff and Catherine at the novel's end. Lockwood is still unaware of the existence of either Isabella or the first Catherine. He finds it hard enough to deal with what lies palpably before him. If Cathy is not Heathcliff's wife but his daughter-in-law she must be married, he surmises, to the un-washed "clown" he assumes to be "Heathcliff, junior." And so Lockwood addresses this bumpkin with another burst of periphrastic language: "Ah, certainly — I see now; you are the favoured possessor of the beneficent fairy."

Once again, a strained attempt at flattery is immediately undermined by an emotional explosion that shatters Lockwood's professions of sincerity. Hareton grows crimson, clenches his fists, and barely stifles some "brutal curse" which his urbane rival awkwardly takes "care not to notice." Just as Lockwood has unintentionally given us our first glimpse into the depths of Heathcliff's attachment to the dead Catherine, so has he now, as unwittingly as before, made us aware of Hareton's powerful love for Catherine's living daughter and namesake. (Following critical practice, I shall call the second Catherine "Cathy" in order to distinguish her from her mother.) Lockwood has therefore managed to stum-ble upon the two male–female relationships which will need to be resolved before the novel can come to a close. For only at the book's end can the unions Lockwood has imagined actually come true. Heathcliff can at last join his Catherine in a numinous reality that lies beyond language, a reality where neither wives nor "amiable ladies" can constrain desire. And the living Cathy can marry Hareton who, by then, has become transformed into a gentleman every bit as amiable as Lockwood.

As long as Lockwood assures himself that someone else is the physical "possessor" of a "beneficent fairy," he can safe-ly toy with his own prospects of possessing a desirable female complement. He tells himself that Cathy, whom he recognizes to be of his own social standing, must have "thrown herself away" on the "repulsive" and inarticulate boor he nonetheless tries so lavishly to flatter. And, flattering himself, Lockwood avows that he must protect his own "susceptible heart" from a Cathy who is bound to recognize him as Hareton's "better." He reminds himself, possibly recalling his sea-side flirtation, that "I knew that I was tolerably attractive." But Brontë makes us see that Lockwood is not destined to play a role in her novel's love-plots. For his charade is shattered as soon as Heathcliff sardonically explains that neither he nor Hareton, who "assuredly" is not his son, has "the privilege of owning your good fairy." Since Heathcliff further volunteers that Cathy's "mate is dead," as dead as the brace of rabbits which Lockwood mistook for living kittens, it would appear that ownership of such a prize is available to any sincere young suitor. The information so disturbs Lockwood that he at last admits that he feels "unmistakably out of place in that pleasant family circle." Despite the whirling snowstorm outside, he soon begs Cathy herself to show him some landmarks by which he might find his way back to the more congenial Grange he calls his "home" (ch. 2).

But Brontë will not permit Lockwood to steal away until she has forced our agent to confront more fully the femininity he wants to evade. In a book in which male and female halves yearn for a psychic integration, Lockwood must be teased with the possibility of "possession," not only of, but also by, a complementary female spirit. If the "ambiguous" pseudonym of "Ellis Bell" was chosen — as Charlotte Brontë explained in her "Biographical Notice" — so that a female author could successfully hide her identity behind a name not "positively masculine," so does Emily Brontë want to strip away the doubtful masculinity of the mask she has adopted in her ironic impersonation of Lockwood. The youth who had boasted of his affinity with his "erect and handsome" landlord (ch. 1) will be given an opportunity to test that affinity by being allowed to encounter the ghost Heathcliff wants to embrace. For not only the girlish widow who seems to be of Lockwood's own age, but also the dead Catherine will materialize, in a stage of development as unformed as the one in which Lockwood is still floundering. Either one of these female counterparts could potentially act as Lockwood's psychological double, the needed complement or epipsyche (to use Shelley's term) which would make his own psyche whole.

Before meeting the ghost of the first Catherine, however, Lockwood finds himself identifying with Cathy through still another one of his misperceptions. When the servant Joseph delivers a tirade in a dialect quite far removed from Lockwood's allusions to a "presiding genius" of home and heart, the thoroughly confused Lockwood becomes convinced that he, rather than Cathy, is the object of the old man's attack. Joseph sputters venomously: "Bud yah're a nowt, and it's noa use talking − yah'll niver mend uh yer ill ways; bud goa raight tuh t'divil, like yer mother afore ye" (ch. 2). Assuming that his own useless talk is being referred to, reduced in his self-esteem as a "nowt" or nothing, Lockwood, the son whose "dear mother" predicted he would never find a home, assumes that "this piece of eloquence was addressed to me," rather than to one far more dispossessed than he. Mentally, he plans some form of masculine retaliation, only to discover that Cathy, the real object of Joseph's hateful address, is fully capable of defending herself. Her strength comes from "a long, dark book" that she takes from a shelf. Posing as a necromancer, the "little witch" − as Lockwood admiringly calls her while observing the "mock malignity" in her "beautiful eyes" − puts Joseph to flight.

What is noteworthy about this identification is its non-sexual nature. Despite his allusion to her "beautiful eyes," Lockwood no longer needs to entertain Cathy as a love-object. Instead, he is entranced by her capacity to outwit the "trembling" Joseph, who rushes away "praying and ejaculating 'wicked' as he went." But Cathy is no more "wicked" than Lockwood himself, whom Joseph will soon falsely accuse of stealing a lantern. Though powerless in a household where she can be abused by a servant, Cathy is capable of turning on her superstitious tormentor through a playfulness that Lockwood describes as a "species of dreary fun." Words, taken from books, need not be sterile and wooden. They can remain vital, activated as weapons that can disarm those nominally in power. Asking for directions to leave the Heights, Lockwood approaches Cathy who has, after her victory over Joseph, begun to read in "the long book open before her." He begs her "to *tell* me my way, not to *show* it." He is referring to the way to the Grange. But Cathy has shown the bookish Lockwood a better way to enlist language. She is as much his potential ally, as the first Catherine was Heathcliff's ally and playmate. For, as Lockwood soon discovers, Joseph the Pharisee, the denier of the biblical Word he invokes so self-righteously and rigidly, was also the antagonist of Cathy's verbally adroit mother.

Lockwood's affinity with a female activator of words becomes even more pronounced when, in chapter 3, he comes upon the "Testament" that bears the inscription, "Catherine Earnshaw, her book." His playful attack, in the first of his two dreams, against the transgressions of male zealots, whose inflexible "discourse" has made him and all other listeners to such religious harangues "fellow martyrs," suggests that he has profited from his identification with the two rebellious Catherines (ch. 3). It is no wonder that he should grapple in his dream "with Joseph, my nearest and most ferocious assailant." Attracted at first by Heathcliff's anti-social behavior only to find himself mocked for his own "sociability," Lockwood finds it easier to identify with the verbal defiance of females even more at home in a world of books than he is. Like Branwell Brontë, whose imagination thrived in the company of his literate sisters, Lockwood seems to prefer the fellowship of the two Catherines to the masculine society of Heathcliff or Hareton.

Still, Lockwood's burgeoning sympathy for the two Catherines will be severely jolted in the second of his two dreams. The "ice-cold hand" of his eerie visitor proves too much of a possession for him to bear. Lockwood the would-be participant becomes Lockwood the reader again, as he piles "books up in a pyramid" as a protective barrier against the female exile who returns to claim her place. His refusal to come under her spell tarnishes his capacity for sympathy and relegates him to the subsidiary role from which he could have emerged. In this novel written by a woman, to resist the invasion of the female is to remain a spectator and outsider. The strange story that Lockwood was on the verge of deciphering must be wrested away from him and assigned to female narrators, Nelly Dean, Isabella Linton, and Catherine Earnshaw herself.

The romantics and Emily Brontë

When F. R. Leavis characterized *Wuthering Heights* as "an astonishing work" that somehow could find no place within his "Great Tradition" of the English novel, he based his judgment on considerations not unlike those which had presumably led mid-Victorian readers to reject Lockwood as their agent. Though respectful of Emily Brontë's "genius," Leavis regarded her work as eccentric, "a kind of sport." The book, he therefore concluded, belonged neither to the "tradition coming down from the eighteenth century that demanded a plane-mirror reflection of the surfaces of 'real' life," nor to the more recent "Scott tradition that imposed on the novelist a romantic resolution of his themes" (*The Great Tradition*, London, 1948). Two assumptions need to be singled out here for further scrutiny. First, even if it were conceded that Emily Brontë "broke" as absolutely with these two "traditions" as Leavis contends she did, her subversion of existing novelistic conventions still has to be closely inspected, since, like all subversions – from Cervantes to Nabokov – such an act of repudiation necessarily encodes the fictional precedents it wants the reader to reject. Even more problematic, however, is the second assumption that the only literary coordinates by which we might gauge our entry into the construct called *Wuthering Heights* can be furnished by other novels. As this section will eventually try to show, there were other "Romantic" constructs besides novels which Brontë fully expected her readers to recognize when she asked them to share Lockwood's opening disorientation.

Superficially at least, Lockwood resembles a figure who had become central to what Leavis calls the "Scott tradition." The young urban outsider who ventures into a more primitive world was a character whom Sir Walter Scott had perfected in the popular novels he wrote from the 1814 *Waverley* to the 1832 *Castle Dangerous*. Hovering between the conflicting realities of city and country, often attracted to a heroine who proves to be far more vital and passionate than her civilized English cousins, this "wavering" hero is manipulated by Scott to bring about some final synthesis of resolution. Just as Lockwood breaks down after his second visit to the Heights and has to be nursed back to health by Nelly Dean in the friendlier atmosphere of Thrushcross Grange, so is the Scott hero, who often is similarly impaired by sickness or by wounds, ultimately repaired and led to adopt a broader outlook. Such conversions became a central feature in the Victorian novel. Other novelists emulated Scott by allowing male naifs to become educated and transformed: David Copperfield finally benefits from the ministrations of Agnes; at the end of *Vanity Fair*, the sadder but wiser Dobbin comes to prefer his little daughter Jane to the woman he has sentimentalized for too long.

Lockwood, however, differs significantly from such prototypes by refusing to become a fully fledged participant in the reality Nelly unfolds for him and, at least initially, invites him to share. For Emily Brontë has no interest whatsoever in converting the man who peeked past the "penetralium" of the Heights. Unlike Scott's Waverley or Darsie, Lockwood must remain a marginal figure. And, since he acts, as we have seen, as the contemporary reader's agent, he only shows how unwilling his creator is to accommodate the values of that reader's culture. Although she will eventually allow Cathy to transform Hareton into a civilized version of Heathcliff, Brontë remains far more doubtful — as we shall see when we reach the book's resolution — about the benefits of this process of domestication than either Scott or the early Dickens would have been. Heathcliff, after all, not Hareton, remains the most memorable figure in *Wuthering Heights*.

Emily Brontë's defiance of what Leavis calls the "Scott tradition" thus is quite calculated. Readers who had been led to expect Lockwood to turn into the hero of his own tale were obviously disappointed to find him displaced by his more anarchic anti-type. The anarchic figures whom Scott or Dickens had opposed to those eventually adhering to a middle road were usually ejected from the world of the novel. Heathcliff, though nominally gone from the book at the end, very much remained to vex the mid-Victorian reader. Charlotte Brontë, Emily's prime reader, testified to that vexation in her "Editor's Preface" when she so extravagantly dubbed him "a man's shape animated by demon life – a Ghoul – an Afreet," and earnestly wondered whether "it is right or advisable to create beings like Heathcliff."

From Scott, to whose *Old Mortality* (1816) and *The Black Dwarf* (1816) her novel bears other specific, though minor, points of resemblance, Emily Brontë also seems to have drawn a sanction for her own use of Yorkshire topography and dialect (spoken by Joseph). But her almost anthropological grounding of the novel in the region she knew best was hardly a limitation, as Charlotte seems to hint when she asserts that a wider literary culture might have helped Emily move beyond the confines of her "native hills." Indeed, *Wuthering Heights* draws on that wider culture. The book's combination of broad comedy with elements of the fantastic yields of generic mix quite similar to that found in German novellas, frequently reviewed and translated in *Blackwood's Magazine*, which the Brontës regularly read. As early as 1857, the French critic Montégut noted similarities between *Wuthering Heights* and the fiction of E. T. A. Hoffmann, notably "Das Majorat" ("The Entail"). That revenge-story, which spans over three generations, features a "morose" Heathcliffian recluse, as well as an eerie and violent re-enactment of a past crime which is witnessed by a narrator who has fallen asleep after reading a copy of Schiller's *Ghost-Seer*. Emily may well have read the story in translation, or even in the original when she was studying German in Brussels. She may also have been familiar with other works of fiction that have been cited as analogues — Hoffmann's own "The Devil's Elixir" (translated in 1824), with its similar opening, and an anonymous Irish tale called "The Bridegroom of Barna" (published in *Blackwood's* in 1840), which (as Leicester Bradner first pointed out in a 1933 essay) contains some striking similarities, notably the exhuming by her former lover of a maiden who died of a chill while roaming the moors.

Still, as suggested earlier, it seems a mistake to limit a search for the literary ancestry of *Wuthering Heights* exclusively in the realm of fiction — a mistake that, in a way, only replicates that of the original readers who, conditioned by Scott, Bulwer, Dickens, and Thackeray, felt thwarted by Emily Brontë's defiance of familiar novelistic conventions. Would her Victorian audience have been more receptive to the boldness of her generic experimentations had they known that she had come to the novel directly from her mastery of lyrical and dramatic verse? Emily was by far the most gifted of the three contributors to the 1846 *Poems by Currer, Ellis, and Acton Bell.* As Charlotte correctly (and generously) intimated in her 1850 "Biographical Notice," the volume might have fared better had it featured only the work of "Ellis Bell." Emily's originality — both in her visionary lyrics and in the powerful dramatic monologues of her Gondal poems — might have more fully stood out and hence been better perceived. Her Gondal saga, reconstructed by Fannie Elizabeth Ratchford in *The Brontës' Web of Childhood* (1941) and *Gondal's Queen* (1955), bears conspicuous resemblances to her novel, discussed by Ratchford and also by Mary Visick in *The Genesis of 'Wuthering Heights'* (1958).

The major coordinates of *Wuthering Heights* must therefore be located elsewhere: the book owes much to its author's command of Shakespeare's poetic drama, and even more to her profound understanding of the poetry and prose of the English Romantics who had themselves adopted Shakespeare (as well as Milton) as one of their own. Indeed, one of the many achievements of *Wuthering Heights* lies in its successful transference to prose fiction of some of the formal strategies and thematic concerns of the Romantic essayists and poets. In this sense, Emily Brontë, though habitually classified as a Victorian novelist, is even more of a third-generation Romantic than Victorian poets such as Tennyson (born nine years before her), Elizabeth Barrett Browning (born twelve years earlier), and Matthew Arnold (born three years later).

Like any major Romantic text, *Wuthering Heights* concerns itself with the operations of the imagination, that creative and recreative faculty which Coleridge defined as "the living power and prime Agent of all human Perception" (*Biographia Literaria*, ch. 13). For Romantic critics like Coleridge, Hazlitt, Lamb, and De Quincey (the latter another contributor to *Blackwood's*, and hence especially well-known to the Brontës), the highest exemplar of that empathetic imagination was Shakespeare. In his famous 1823 essay "On the Knocking at the Gate in *Macbeth*" De Quincey analyzed the means by which Shakespeare overcomes the spectator's horror over Duncan's murder and compels us, instead, to identify with the "hell within" the minds of the murderers. *Wuthering Heights* carefully deploys its allusions to *Macbeth* (even the "brindled" cat that calms Lockwood of the murderous feelings he had experienced "when I had no longer my imagination under control" [ch. 3] provides a deftly-placed cross-reference to the play). Ghosts, possession, monomania, usurpation, brutality and revenge upon innocents, are woven into the fabric of a tale told, if not by an idiot, then at least by a foolish young man who is made to feel like one. And Heathcliff and Catherine are eventually "taken out" − to use De Quincey's phrase about Macbeth and his Lady − "of the region of human things, human purposes, human desires."

That the affinities between *Macbeth* and Brontë's novel did not wholly escape the early readers of *Wuthering Heights* is borne out by a recently discovered American review of June 1848. The reviewer (whom Albert J. von Frank identifies as one Charles Briggs) went against the received opinion of the times by vowing: "Excepting *Macbeth* and [Scott's] *Bride of Lammermoor*, we have never opened a book so full of the elements of genuine tragedy as *Wuthering Heights*." He went on to expound upon the analogies he perceived: "There is the same kind of dread interest in *Wuthering Heights*, which so fastens upon one in *Macbeth* and the *Bride of Lammermoor*, in the beginning of those terrifying tragedies. You feel that you are about to witness the realisation of some dread decree of fate which fascinates your attention, while you shudder to anticipate it." As this remark seems to confirm, our entrance into *Wuthering Heights* draws us into a dynamic similar to that which De Quincey so brilliantly analyzed as operating in *Macbeth*.

In "The Knocking at the Gate in *Macbeth*," De Quincey shows how Shakespeare makes us sympathize with a demonism that remains "locked up" and "cut off" from "the world of ordinary life" that lies beyond Macbeth's castle. His remarks have an important bearing on a novel that demands, as much as Shakespeare's play, that we overcome our potential antipathy towards an obsessed and ruthless protagonist. De Quincey suggests that we succumb to the dreamlike abolition of time within the walled structure; but he also insists that, as soon as the knocking is heard by the spectator, we awake from our state of hypnotic torpor and are restored to the "normal pulses of life." Brontë relies on a similar rhythm in *Wuthering Heights*, where our involvement with Heathcliff must give way to the more ordinary "pulses" represented by Hareton and Cathy, the nurslings of Nelly Dean. Yet she also makes involvement with Heathcliff more difficult. It is easier to identify with the Scottish thane we see becoming infected by the three weird sisters at the very outset of the play than with the mysterious Mr. Heathcliff so imperfectly glimpsed by Lockwood in the first chapters of the book. Even observers more closely placed to Heathcliff will shun him as a "ghoul" or "demon." And although they witness his agonies, Nelly and Isabella remain remarkably aloof from the figure Emily's own two sisters repudiated.

Even more than in *Macbeth*, "sympathy" in *Wuthering Heights* depends on the cooperating imagination of those outside the story. Whereas De Quincey treats the intrusive knocking at the gate as a welcome restoration of the ordinary, Brontë begins her novel with the ordinary Lockwood's unwelcome intrusion. The "gate" over which Heathcliff leans, we are told, manifests no "sympathizing movement"; although Lockwood jumps over the gate's chain on his second visit, he complains about having "knocked vainly for admittance, till my knuckles tingled and the dogs howled" (ch. 2). The massive door, with the date "1500," finally opens and yields an inner space in which an obliterated temporality gives way to dream and myth. Like Macbeth's castle, the Heights is a bastion where, in De Quincey's words, ordinary clock-time becomes "suddenly arrested, laid asleep, tranced, racked into a dread armistice." The swirling snow storm erases all the markers Lockwood noted on his second trip to the Heights. As he stumbles back to the normalcy of the Grange, he remarks that all the sign-posts "which my yesterday's walk left pictured in my mind" have been "blotted" by the "billowy, white ocean" (ch. 3). Sympathy, Lockwood has by now discovered, can be dangerous. The boundaries of our individuality can be lost in the full merger by which we enter another's feelings (or dreams). As De Quincey notes: "time must be annihilated, relation to things without abolished; and all must pass self-withdrawn into a deeper syncope and suspension of earthly passion."

In *Macbeth*, the spectator who fends off pain and horror by withdrawing an ordinary sympathy *for* Duncan the victim and transforming it into a sympathy *with* Macbeth the murderer, can awake from that imaginative complicity through the knocking at the porter's gate. In *Wuthering Heights*, however, Brontë carries this process of identification one step further when she has Lockwood, our agent, experience a dream intended for Heathcliff. Lockwood, too, hears a knocking during his state of suspended disbelief. This sound does not come from the ordinary life without, but rather from an extraordinary apparition which, like Banquo's ghost, demands to be recognized by a terrified imagination. In his violent response to the ghost's proffered hand, Lockwood becomes as blood-bespattered as Macbeth, yet refuses to be possessed by the fantastic creature he has animated. And, in a further reversal of the rhythm of *Macbeth*, the figure who now rushes in to confront the awakened Lockwood is not an emissary of the normal "goings-on of the world" but rather Heathcliff himself. Whereas Lockwood, like the spectator of *Macbeth*, is eager to recover his detachment, Heathcliff wants to recover the intensity of the fusion Lockwood has rejected. Heathcliff's histrionic behavior now disturbs Lockwood, for whom all dramatic illusion has vanished. While Heathcliff grinds his teeth, crushes "his nails into his palms," and strikes "his forehead with rage," Lockwood assumes the stance of a suddenly indifferent viewer, preoccupied with more mundane matters. He resumes his "toilette rather noisily," he informs us, "looked at my watch, and soliloquized on the length of the night." Like a bored play-goer, he observes, "Time stagnates here." Lockwood no longer wants any part of the mythic dream-world, "swarming with ghosts and goblins," into which he had stumbled. He is ready for the measured "history" that now awaits him: Nelly Dean's neatly linear narrative.

At the beginning of his essay, De Quincey points out that, as long as he had "obstinately" endeavoured "with my understanding to comprehend this," he remained unable to account for the knocking which follows Duncan's murder. He blames this deficiency on his having relied upon the wrong "faculty" of mind: any "understanding, which includes no *intuitive knowledge* of the laws of vision," he contends, must remain incomplete (the added emphasis is mine). The distinction De Quincey here sets up between "intuition" and "understanding" – which he shared with other Romantics – has a significant bearing on *Wuthering Heights*, where Lockwood's "understanding" cannot process what his imagination has intuitively unlocked in the second of his dreams. But the division not only separates Lockwood from

Heathcliff, who longs for the spectral visit Lockwood has
rejected; it also sets Nelly Dean apart from Catherine Earnshaw, and, even more importantly, it marks Catherine's own
split between Edgar Linton and Heathcliff. The very form of
the novel, its repetitions and dualisms, its clashing modes of
speech and its persistent appeal to two very different kinds of
perception, result from aims very similar to those shaping the
experimental prose and poetry of the English Romantics.

I have relied on De Quincey's short essay rather than on
other major Romantic texts because of its representativeness
and compactness. There is one link, however, which cannot
be made through "The Knocking at the Gate in *Macbeth*,"
– namely Emily Brontë's adaptation of the Romantic quest
for a female complement desired by a male seeker. Wordsworth's repeated efforts to treat his "dear, dear Sister" as a
compensation for the loss of his childhood oneness with a
feminine Nature, Coleridge's own recollection of his sisterly
"play-mate when we were both clothed alike," Byron's more
erotic apostrophes to his half-sister and his incestual sug-
gestions in *Manfred*, Lamb's rejection of a sexual union in
favor of the partnership offered by the sister he fictionalized
into the "unchanged" and "faithful" Bridget of Elia's essays
– all these, and many more, are of particular relevance to a
fiction about sororal and fraternal selves, a tale written by an
author whose creativity was first activated through childhood
play with her siblings.

Although I shall occasionally refer to other Romantic correlatives, four texts might be briefly singled out here for their
special importance to Emily Brontë's concern with the loss
and recovery of the childhood oneness of male and female
halves. The first two are a poem and a novel: Percy Shelley's
"Epipsychidion" (1821) and Mary Shelley's *Frankenstein*
(first published in 1818 and revised, in the version Emily
undoubtedly read, in 1831). The other two are works of non-
fictional prose and, once again, by De Quincey: *Confessions
of an English Opium-Eater* (1822) and *Recollections of the
Lake Poets* (serialized from 1834 to 1840 in *Tait's Magazine*,
another journal read regularly by the Brontës).

Edward Chitham begins *A Life of Emily Brontë* (1987) with an epigraph drawn from Percy Shelley's "Epipsychidion." The lines are indeed startling:

> Emily,
> I love thee; though the world by no thin name
> Will hide that love from its unvalued shame.
> Would we two had been twins of the same mother!
> Or, that the name my heart leant to another
> Could be a sister's bond for her and thee,
> Blending two beams of one eternity!
> Yet were one lawful and the other true,
> These names, though dear, could paint not, as is due,
> How beyond refuge I am thine. Ah me!
> I am not thine: I am a part of thee.   (lines 42–52)

Chitham suggests that the poem in which Shelley so fervently addresses another Emily − Emilia Viviani − as his "heart's sister" acquired a special poignancy for a writer who shared Shelley's uncompromising idealism. Basing his claim on such poems as the 1839 lyric "Shed No Tears O'er That Tomb," Chitham concludes that a man "long ago" dead, whom Emily sometimes links in other verses to her dead sisters Maria and Elizabeth and at other times treats as a still defiant shade, was Shelley himself. If so, the identification can be extended to *Wuthering Heights*, where Catherine tells Nelly that her soul and Heathcliff's "are the same," whether or not she is lawfully married to Edgar Linton. Heathcliff's own desire for consummation with his dead soul-sister in what Catherine describes as "an existence of yours beyond you" is itself quintessentially Shelleian (ch. 9). The search for a single "Spirit within two frames" is as central to *Wuthering Heights* as it is to "Epipsychidion" or to Shelley's earlier poem "Alastor."

But to convert his idealized Emily into a "soul out of my soul" or "Epipsyche," Percy Shelley also was forced to shed the woman who carried his legal name, Mary Shelley, and imagine "a sister's bond for her and thee." Mary's own *Frankenstein*, which had gained a much wider audience upon its first appearance than did either Shelley's poems or *Wuthering Heights*, depicts the price women must pay for the

Promethean defiance of idealists such as Percy or his friend Byron. Elizabeth Lavenza, whom Victor Frankenstein welcomes to his parents' home, as "my more than sister" (1831), will be destroyed by the creature he animates. Like the single-named Heathcliff, this nameless being becomes a revengeful male sadist when denied a sister-bride, "a companion of the same nature as myself." Women and children are the prime victims in each novel. Thwarted in their own child-like yearning for a female other, both Heathcliff and Frankenstein's creature resent their own socialization. Catherine refuses to extend "pity" to Heathcliff, whom she accuses of having killed her, "and thriven on it" (ch. 15). For her part, Isabella wishes that the husband she calls "Monster" might "be blotted out of creation" (ch. 17). Brontë's women differ from Mary Shelley's passive female martyrs. Whereas Justine and Elizabeth are immolated by a Frankenstein Monster who insists that he, whose "heart was fashioned to be susceptible of love and sympathy," would have preferred to remain as passive as his victims, the two Catherines and Isabella match the adult Heathcliff's aggressiveness. Catherine wrangles with Heathcliff on her very deathbed. She assures him that she will share his "distress" once underground. His final decision to join her thus differs from the Frankenstein creature's self-immolation. Though both Heathcliff and the Monster will their own deaths, the former's hope of reunion with the epipsyche who haunted him removes all his previous bitterness. Bereft of a double, Shelley's creature remains as alienated in death as he was in life.

Unlike his essay on *Macbeth*, De Quincey's *Confessions of an English Opium-Eater*, which also contrasts "discursive understanding" to fantasy, is shaped by the narrator's search for a lost sister-figure. Sought in the actuality of the "labyrinths of London" his memory revisits, she is eventually relocated in dreamscapes induced by opium as a creature of the imagination. The work undoubtedly had a special significance for Emily Brontë, who would have associated it with her brother Branwell. The young man who saw himself as a latter-day Romantic child regarded De Quincey's *Confessions* as a testament of his own aspirations, as Winifred Gérin shows in her *Branwell Brontë* (1961). Addicted to the same "divine elixir" to which De Quincey had resorted to recover femininity lost, Branwell was similarly obsessed with the recovery of a lost sister. His fixation on the dead Maria Brontë, the extraordinary eldest child who had nursed her siblings after Mrs Brontë's death, found an analogue in De Quincey's discussion of his own involvement with a ghost-child in the last installment of his *Recollections of the Lake Poets*. This account appeared in 1840, the year in which Branwell traveled to the Lake Country to introduce himself to Hartley Coleridge and three decades after De Quincey had removed himself from the stir of society in order to live in the vicinity of the Wordsworth and Coleridge families.

De Quincey ends his *Recollections* by recreating the hallucinations he experienced in his grief over the death of little Kate Wordsworth, the poet's three-year-old daughter, a playmate who "walked with me, slept with me, and was my sole companion." The vivid description of her apparition over the grave on which he stretched himself "for more than two months running" not only has a bearing on Branwell's efforts to keep alive the memory of little Maria, but also is highly relevant both to Lockwood's second dream and to his concluding insistence on the quieted graveyard. Though produced by a "frenzy of grief" much like that which Heathcliff exhibits, the dream-child who appears to De Quincey evokes none of Lockwood's frenzied resistance. She is welcomed as a natural phantom of delight:

usually I saw her at the opposite side of the field, which might sometimes be at a distance of a quarter of a mile, generally not so much. Always almost she carried a basket on her head; and usually the first hint upon which the figure arose commenced in wild plants, such as tall ferns, or the purple flowers of the foxglove; but, whatever might be the colours or the forms, uniformly the same little full-formed figure arose, uniformly dressed in the little blue bed-gown and black skirt of Westmoreland, and uniformly with the air of advancing motion.   ("Society of the Lakes − V")

Like Lockwood, however, or like the spectator of *Macbeth*

who shakes off the demonic, De Quincey eventually ceases to be possessed by this sprite. Like Lockwood after the visitation of his dream, he now falls ill, so "debilitated" that he can hardly stand up. He leaves the area for several months (as Lockwood does after chapter 31). And when he returns he finds, not only that the ghost will not return, but also that he can no longer remember the child's actual features. He has repressed an image which "had, with my malady, vanished from my mind." The grave which he revisits "was looked at almost with indifference." A Heathcliff yearning for Catherine Wordsworth has become a Lockwood who can think of no unquiet sleepers and who falls back on common "understanding" to classify his experience as a psychological case-study that may confirm "the old Pagan superstition of a nympholepsy." This Catherine, too, has been laid to rest.

Chapter 2

The narrative structures of *Wuthering Heights*

Order and Instability

Just as the thick-walled "dwelling" Lockwood twice penetrates in the first three chapters proves less secure than he expected it to be, so does the structure of *Wuthering Heights* thwart the reader's expectations of stability. The form of the novel has often been likened to that of a series of Chinese boxes-within-boxes or to that of a many-layered onion (a form which the book shares with earlier Romantic narratives such as *Frankenstein* or "The Eve of St. Agnes"). Any one container or enveloping layer, when pried open or stripped, only yields a further receptacle which, in turn, offers still another closed container. Emily Brontë calls attention to this format when she allows Lockwood to venture into the "little closet" in the room to which he has been led by Zillah.

When Lockwood enters the "large oak case" and finds a bed within its shell, the man who had earlier compared himself to a snail welcomes the insulation that this snug "structure" would seem to offer him. After his mistakes and humiliation, he sorely needs a stable refuge. Lockwood's sense of security is strengthened when he notices that one of the closet's sides leans against "the ledge of a window," the clasp of which has been firmly "soldered into the staple" (ch. 3). Whereas this side of the enclosure rests against the protective outer wall of the building, the other three appear to be just as impenetrable: each thick panel, topped only by cut-out squares that resemble "coach windows," helps to shelter the occupant. Lockwood basks in the illusory privacy offered by this self-contained unit in a dwelling which, though much larger than the cramped quarters to which the Brontë family were confined at Haworth, still remains too small to allow the luxury "for every member of the family of having a room to himself" (ch. 3).

Yet Lockwood soon becomes a mental traveler in this stationary room-within-a-room. The unexpected voyages he takes as a dreamer break down the barriers of space and time and even those of gender. He fights off and aborts his second dream precisely because it threatens to abolish the barriers he requires for his mental stability. Lockwood thus deprives us of a chance of reaching the center of this novel of husks and containers. We are forced to join him in his retreat. From the hearth in the "back-kitchen," where he spends the remainder of the night with the cat as his "companion," Lockwood flees to the comforts of an even more "companionable" structure at Thrushcross Grange (chs, 3, 4). There, where he can "crouch" next to the crackling fire of still another domestic hearth, his over-stimulated "nerves and brain" must be soothed by a gradual reinstatement of the sequential and hierarchical order that his encounter with a ghost had so severely dislocated (ch. 4).

At the Grange Lockwood gratefully yields to a story-teller better equipped to manage a narrative that was about to become as confusing to the reader as to himself. On the surface, Nelly Dean's tidy arrangement of events would seem to supply us with the ordering devices we have so far lacked. The "sensible" woman whom Lockwood hopes to find a "regular gossip" (ch. 4) has direct access to the missing details which made Lockwood's own first-hand account so tentative and disjointed. But even though Nelly allows us to fit the story's fragments into a more coherent whole, Brontë still suggests that this teller's narrative sequence, though wider in compass, more sustained, and better organized, has severe limits of its own. Thus, Nelly lacks important information about the boy Heathcliff's origins and about the means by which the returning "Mr. Heathcliff" was able to shed all "marks of former degradation" (ch. 10). Even at the outset of her narrative, Nelly is denied knowledge of what the reader has already so fully shared with Lockwood. On learning that Lockwood has visited the Heights, she wants to know how he found "Miss Cathy." But Lockwood never apprises her of his acquaintance with the first Catherine, whose diary he has read. And he conceals from Nelly the impact which that rival female narrative, "scrawled in an unformed, childish hand" (ch. 3), has had on his imagination.

By asking her readers, rather than the inquisitive Nelly Dean, to share Lockwood's terrified contact with "the fingers of a little, ice-cold hand," Brontë reminds us that none of her witnesses can aspire to the total knowledge which the implied author at best allows us to approximate. The various narratives – Lockwood's and Nelly's, Catherine's and Cathy's, Heathcliff's and Isabella's – remain partial strands. It devolves on the reader to reconcile such strands – or to notice their resistance to reconciliation. Nelly's account helps to explain much that confused Lockwood. But her adherence to what is palpable is offset by strange manifestations she fears as much as he does. Lockwood's irrational, achronological dream-encounter with a roaming child who claims to have been "a waif for twenty years" cannot blend with the mostly commonsensical, chronological sequence devised by a middle-aged woman who prides herself on having resisted the same Catherine's dreams. Though more capacious as a container than Lockwood's, Nelly's narrative only compels us to reopen the box labelled "Lockwood's Dream."

This chapter will dwell on five distinct ways in which Emily Brontë arranges the story-elements we need to master before we can fully interpret their significance. These materials are mostly presented through the agency of Brontë's primary, yet limited, surrogate, the "sensible" Mrs. Dean, who will try to impress on them her own point of view. The five categories are: (1) the genealogy or ancestral pedigree of the book's main characters; (2) the chronology of events that go back in time more than thirty years before Lockwood visits the Heights but which also move forward in time for more than a year after his arrival; (3) the rhythm created by the order in which tellers other than Lockwood and Nelly intervene in the story; (4) the rhythm created through the placement of characters at either the Heights or the Grange and by the movement between these localities; (5) the rhythm created by the use of repetition and duplication. Whenever appropriate, we will also consider some significant omissions or deviations from these patterns of order.

The five categories discussed below take into account the novel's remarkable fluidity. We can at last range over the entire text. Whereas the preceding chapter remained anchored, with Lockwood, at the main action's outer periphery, we can now look far beyond the "penetralium" he crossed only to flee again. Still, this chapter will try as much as possible to delay a full interpretation. We must understand how the novel's ordering devices operate before we can start to assess its import. The *meanings* these devices introduce – whether these be the meanings injected by biased tellers such as Nelly or the meanings imbedded by an implied author who teases us by her elusiveness – cannot receive our attention until the third, interpretive, chapter of this study.

Lineage and non-lineage

Identity is determined by genealogy – the record of one's ancestry and kin. Lockwood first queries Nelly about the "history" of the three people he has met at the Heights: he asks, in succession, about "that pretty girl-widow," "that Earnshaw," and that "rough fellow," Heathcliff. Having seen the name "'Earnshaw' carved over the front door," Lockwood has correctly surmised that the rustic youth he saw must somehow belong to "an old family." But given Cathy's refinement, he has assumed that she might not be "a native of the country." Instead, he discovers that she is as indigenous as Hareton, having been born and raised at the Grange while still going by her maiden name of Linton (a name Lockwood recognizes as the one also used by his dream's visitor, "my ghostly Catherine"). Only about the ancestry of the third inhabitant, Heathcliff, whom Lockwood assumed to be as local a fixture as Hareton, does Nelly's information seem notoriously scanty. To Lockwood's question, "Do you know anything of his history?," she replies: 'It's a cuckoo's, sir − I know all about it, except where he was born, and who were his parents, and how he got his money, at first" (ch. 4).

Each of the figures about whom Lockwood has inquired thus represents one of the three groups that interact with the other two in the plot of *Wuthering Heights*: there are the Earnshaws associated with the ancient, wind-battered structure of the Heights; there are the Lintons associated with the more recently built, sheltered country-house of the Grange; and there are the three outsiders imported by the Earnshaw masters: Nelly, Heathcliff, and Frances. The Earnshaws and Lintons *have* a "history" which the novel will continue to propel; the unaffiliated outsiders contribute to that forward movement, but their own ancestry, and hence their status, remain murky. A diagram can give us a schematic overview of the relations among these three groups. There are three generations of Earnshaws and Lintons portrayed in the novel. The three outsiders belong to the age group of the second generation, yet two of them, Nelly and Heathcliff, are more instrumental in shaping the destinies of Hareton and Cathy, the children belonging to the third generation of Earnshaws and Lintons, than were their actual parents. The relations, in diagram form, would look like this:

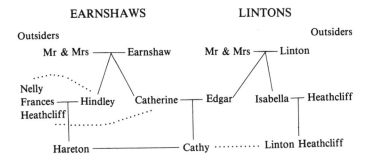

As the lowest line of this diagram reveals, the interaction of the outsiders with the Earnshaws and Lintons results chiefly in the revitalizing of the Earnshaw stock. Whereas the male Linton child, whom Isabella bears Heathcliff, dies before he can consummate his marriage to Cathy, Hareton Earnshaw becomes the scion of the family that traces back its lineage to the founder (or genearch) who bore his own name. Although Frances, Hindley's tubercular bride, died in childbirth, her son proves sturdy enough to grow up without the benefit of mother's milk (a major feat in the late eighteenth century). Hareton is bottle-fed by Nelly Dean who, as the daughter of Hindley's own wet-nurse, has felt closer to Hindley than to his sister Catherine. What is more, Hareton's strong constitution even seems to have benefited from the hardships imposed on him by Heathcliff. Cathy's second husband thus seems to be the prime beneficiary of all three groups: he inherits his vitality from the paternal Earnshaw line; he is formed by three outsiders: Frances (his natural mother), Nelly (who replaces Frances when he is still a small child), and Heathcliff (who replaces Hindley as the boy grows into manhood); lastly, he is civilized by the Linton cousin who helps him to become master of both houses.

The Linton clan also can be said to be strengthened by its interactions with the hardier Earnshaws. Whereas the elder Lintons are so vulnerable that they die upon coming in contact with the sick Catherine, their grand-daughter Cathy — who is half-Earnshaw — is strong enough to overcome the deprivations forced on her by Heathcliff. Although Cathy's courageous defiance of Heathcliff has been anticipated by Isabella Linton, she can withstand hardship more readily than either Isabella or Linton Heathcliff, Isabella's sickly son by Heathcliff. Finding her Earnshaw cousin superior to his debilitated counterpart, Cathy — the blonde daughter of the blond Edgar Linton — wisely insists on taking Hareton away from the Heights back to her father's own estate. The cousin-lovers who had earlier been content to import plants from the Grange to the Heights can now replenish the Linton orchards.

Among the three outsiders, only Frances has a surviving

issue in Hareton. Heathcliff's son by Isabella is too weak to live; Nelly remains single, even though she acts as a surrogate mother to both Hareton and Cathy, her two nurslings. Even more problematic are the origins of these three outsiders. We are told that Hindley brought Frances back with him upon returning from the university to attend his father's funeral. Nelly contends that the existence of this "wife" only "set the neighbours gossiping," for her station and birthplace are kept a secret by Hindley: "What she was, and where she was born he never informed us; probably, she had neither money nor name to recommend her, or he would scarcely have kept the union from his father" (ch. 6). Hindley's devotion to the young woman whom Nelly calls "hysterical" and "half silly" seems sexual, as Catherine had noted in the diary read by Lockwood.

Nelly's status is also veiled. Lockwood has maintained that "her own affairs . . . could hardly interest me" (ch. 4), but these affairs prove to be most intricately intertwined with those of the two families she knows so well. Nelly identifies with the Grange dwellers: when she speaks of "us," she quickly adds, "I mean, of the Lintons" (ch. 4). Yet despite her Linton allegiances, her original ties are unquestionably to the Heights. We know that Nelly's mother was a local woman who nursed her own child and Hindley Earnshaw. There is no allusion to a father. Is "Dean" a paternal or a maternal name? What exactly is Nelly's position in the Earnshaw home in which she, but apparently not her mother, continues to live? Before he offers Heathcliff to his wife as "a gift of God," old Earnshaw had treated Nelly almost as one of his own children (after agreeing to bring Hindley a fiddle and Catherine a whip, he had at least promised Nelly "a pocketful of apples and pears"). Small wonder that Nelly tries to remove this alien child, hoping that it will retreat into the unknown regions from which Earnshaw has hauled it. But the child creeps to the door of the old man who soon prefers Heathcliff to all the other youngsters in his household.

Nelly and Heathcliff thus hold a similar position in the Earnshaw household. The patriarch who asks his protesting wife to give the "name of a son who died in childhood" to the "dirty, ragged, black-haired child" he has brought home from Liverpool, takes to the boy "strangely," according to Nelly (ch. 4), even though he seems to deny him the Earnshaw surname. Could Nelly, who loves Hindley as a brother, and Heathcliff, who is hated by Hindley "as a usurper of his parent's affections and his privileges," possibly both be the illegitimate offspring of old Earnshaw? And, if so, could Nelly's hostility to the first Catherine stem from envy of a status that can never be her own? Hindley's need to find a sexual mate who does not belong to the local gentry thus would not only be an act of defiance of his father but also an act of emulation. And Heathcliff's hatred of Hindley, like Nelly's resentment of Cathy, would revolve around questions of legitimacy. Like Shakespeare's Edmund, Heathcliff will be obsessed by his desire to topple the "legitimate" and to obtain the power from which he is legally debarred. (The novel's many allusions to *King Lear*, as well as the use of the name "Edgar" for the Linton heir whom Heathcliff will also want to displace, seem pertinent here.)

We need not carry such speculations further at this point, except to say that the possibilities they open may have contributed to the shocked response of those Victorian reviewers who deplored the novel's "crude" content. Significantly, the two characters most capable of affecting the destinies of Earnshaws and Lintons lack the legitimacy conferred by genealogical descent. Nelly can allude to a mother. Heathcliff appears to have no recollection of any parent other than the man who adopts him as his own. When the boy appears on the scene, he is already old "enough both to walk and talk," yet he can merely "repeat over and over again some gibberish that nobody could understand" (ch. 4). Like similar figures of interest to the Victorian imagination – Carlyle's Diogenes Teufelsdroeckh in *Sartor Resartus*, for instance, or Tennyson's version of King Arthur in *Idylls of the King* – Heathcliff is the Child from Nowhere. The boy with the single name may be a gipsy (a figure which fascinated nineteenth-century writers) or "a regular black," as Nelly at one point suggests (ch. 7). In trying to reconcile Heathcliff to his unknown identity, Nelly even loosens her habitual realism by concocting a fairy tale heritage: "You're fit for a prince in disguise. Who knows but your father was Emperor of China, and your mother an Indian queen, each of them able to buy up, with one week's income, Wuthering Heights and Thrushcross Grange together?" (ch. 7). Though well-intentioned, Nelly here implants her own concern with property and power in the boy who will return as a man fully capable of appropriating both the Heights and the Grange. The systems of kinship which eventually work even for Nelly Dean will nonetheless fail Heathcliff, whoever he is and from wherever he comes. Like the "cuckoo" with whom Nelly identifies him, he will take possession of nests not his own only to discover the meaninglessness of such a nesting place for one like him.

Chronologies and deviations

Emily Brontë devises different time schemes to suit the different subjectivities of her characters. We have noted before how Lockwood resorts to his watch to counter the "irregular" gasps of a distraught Heathcliff who has thrown himself on the spot where Catherine's ghost had materialized. Embarrassed, Lockwood starts to "soliloquize" on the length of the night: "Not three o'clock yet! I could have taken oath it had been six. Time stagnates here" (ch. 3). Lockwood wants time to speed up; Heathcliff wants to retard or arrest it. The regularity of the ticking watch grasped by Lockwood thus clashes with the "irregular and intercepted breathing" of the man who hopes to push back the clock to an earlier period of freedom and timelessness experienced by Catherine and himself. Yet even that atemporal experience − recaptured in a dream that managed to erase the passage of twenty years − is anchored in time, located in a distinct phase of Catherine's and Heathcliff's development − a phase which seems but a miniscule interlude in the much longer Earnshaw history. The novel's chronologies thus contribute to the Chinese-box effect discussed at the start of this chapter: our own temporal progress as readers of Lockwood's outer narrative enfolds "Lockwood time," which in turn absorbs and condenses "Earnshaw time," Nelly's chronicle of the history of three generations. And, in the innermost container is something akin to what Wordsworth called "spots of time" in his layered poem, *The Prelude*: vivid moments of "distinct pre-eminence" can be traced back to "our first childhood," but are retained in adult memory as reminders of the child's feelings of emancipation from time (1850 *Prelude* XIII, ll. 209, 225).

These conflicting temporal orders are so intricately interwoven that the chronological arrangement of the novel's events which C. P. Sanger undertook in his seminal 1926 essay on "The Structure of *Wuthering Heights*" (reprinted in the Norton edition of the novel) tends to flatten what the reader inevitably experiences as multiple chronologies. The single "Chronology" which Sanger restored has therefore been modified (and abridged) in the version (first devised by Masao Miyoshi) which I reprint at the beginning of this study. Like the ensuing discussion, it stresses the intersection of different time schemes by intersplicing "Lockwood time" with the order followed in Nelly's narrative. Sanger's essay, however, as well as his fuller chronology (which begins in 1757, the year of birth of Hindley Earnshaw and his foster sister, Nelly Dean), should also be consulted for its meticulous reconstruction of the dates which Emily Brontë worked out so precisely but nearly always presents through indirection.

The novel's opening date, "1801 –," and the number "1500" which Lockwood glimpses on entering the Heights, help to remind us of the need to remain alert to the confluence of different chronologies in *Wuthering Heights*. The stops and starts that mark Nelly's telling of the first half of her story, and Lockwood's occasional interruptions, make the reader as time-conscious as the characters themselves. We are not allowed to forget our dependence on Nelly: flattered by Lockwood's compliments of her narrative skills, she decides not to skip three years nor to omit even more of the period

that preceded Catherine's and Heathcliff's separation (ch. 7).
At other times, however, the self-consciousness of teller and
listener has been so fully suspended that the reader is jolted
as much as Lockwood to discover that the pressures of time
force Nelly to halt her story. Like a Scheherazade who knows
how suspense can be heightened by postponement, Nelly
abruptly defers the "sequel of her narrative" right after she
has finished her account of the crucial episode in which
Heathcliff runs away from Catherine. The episode (which
in itself marks the end of a period in which the children
managed to evade the pressures of temporal change) so
engrossed Nelly and the spell-bound Lockwood that they only
now become aware of "the time-piece over the chimney" (ch.
9). Amazed to find that "the minute-hand measure" shows
half-past one, Nelly refuses to go on. Lockwood himself
welcomes the respite that allows him to meditate "for another
hour or so" before dozing off (ch. 9).

The scene acts almost as a set of authorial directions for the
reader's own observance of the clock. It marks off an installment in our reading that is as emphatic as the end of a verse
paragraph would be in our progress through a poem. Our
march through this novel, an implied author seems to suggest,
might be profitably halted at this point. Like Lockwood both
now and on his earlier pausing after absorbing the child
Catherine's diary, we might want to mull over the information we have received before moving on. Still, no literal
curtailment of our reading time is called for, such as that
enforced on the original readers of a serialized novel like
Vanity Fair. (The twelfth monthly number of Thackeray's
book had just appeared when *Wuthering Heights* was
published in December of 1847.)

In her manipulation of the temporal self-consciousness of
her implied audience, Brontë nonetheless produces effects
that are every bit as complicated as those which Thackeray
created through the stops and starts of his own time-obsessed
novel. Indeed, it could be argued that she actually goes
beyond Thackeray's experiments with time. The time-
burdened Showman of *Vanity Fair* compels us to share a

reality in which sober hindsight ultimately remains the only possible ordering device for human bearings. Emily Brontë, on the other hand, mixes her competing chronologies – "Lockwood time" and what we might call Nelly Dean's "Earnshaw Chronicle" – with the essentially achronological reality that Heathcliff wants to recover. *Wuthering Heights* thus becomes a dramatic working-out of the conflict between the temporal progressions it depicts and a timelessness it refuses to sacrifice.

Even without our added awareness of a third time scheme contained in the Heathcliff/Catherine interlude of childhood oneness, the intersection between "Lockwood time" and Nelly's "Earnshaw Chronicle" creates frictions that work against their blending into a single chronology. By the end of chapter 30, such a fusion at last seems possible. Having moved her narrative (chs. 4–30) from an account of Heathcliff's first arrival to the Heights in the summer of 1771 to the successive deaths of Edgar Linton and Linton Heathcliff in September and October of 1801, Nelly has furnished Lockwood with the events that preceded his own arrival in the area in November of 1801. Six weeks of "Lockwood time" have elapsed while she has covered thirty years of the "Earnshaw Chronicle." From this point on in the novel, the calendars can be synchronized, as we move from mid-January of 1802 to the expected union of Cathy and Hareton on New Year's day of 1803.

But the synchronicity does not allow a full blending between "Lockwood time" and Earnshaw/Linton time. For, as soon as Nelly has brought him up to date at the end of chapter 30, Lockwood decides not to stay in the area any longer. No longer desirous of solitude, the young man decides to "spend the next six months in London"; nor does he have any intention of returning to the Grange at any later point of his lease, which expires in October (ch. 30). He travels to the Heights (for the first time since the visit that ended with his illness) in chapter 31. His new encounter with the three inhabitants there is important, for it allows us to detect subtle changes which could not have been observed by Nelly Dean, whom Heathcliff had barred from the Heights three months before. And, what is more, Lockwood's third entry into the Heights dashes any lingering expectation that we might have had of his taking an active part in the concluding installment of the "Earnshaw Chronicle" that still lies before us.

Nelly has ended her version of the "Earnshaw Chronicle" with a barely disguised plea for Lockwood's active intervention. Cathy, she tells Lockwood, will continue to remain Heathcliff's prisoner, "unless," she coyly adds, "she could marry again; and that scheme, it does not come within my province to arrange" (ch. 30). Nelly has clearly detected Lockwood's interest in "that pretty girl-widow." Despite her protestations to the contrary, Cathy's former nurse is not above playing the role of match-maker. She does not know – as we do – about Lockwood's mismanagement of his earlier amorous affair. Nelly therefore offers Lockwood an opportunity to step into the chronological development she has retraced for his benefit. By wresting Cathy away from her confinement at the Heights, the young man could alter events and impress a wholly new direction on the Earnshaw/Linton genealogy, while Nelly would regain her lost influence.

That Nelly's hints have not gone unperceived by Lockwood is clear from his behavior when he revisits the Heights in chapter 31. He satisfies himself that Cathy's "disregard" for him remains as pronounced as it had been: "'She does not seem so amiable'. I thought, 'as Mrs. Dean would persuade me to believe. She's a beauty, it is true; but not an angel'" (ch. 31). Lockwood also observes Cathy's repulsion of Hareton's clumsy attempts to endear himself to her; he even sides with the "manual check" (a slap!) Hareton gives "to her saucy tongue." Contradicting his earlier statements about his own irresistibility, Lockwood is more than happy to cede Cathy to a rival by claiming that a woman who lives "among clowns and misanthropists" would hardly be able to appreciate the "better class of people" to which he belongs. He retreats with evident self-satisfaction over his having refused to become enmeshed in the "Earnshaw Chronicle" as scripted by Nelly: "'How dreary life gets over in that house!'

I reflected, while riding down the road. 'What a realization of something more romantic than a fairy tale it would have been for Mrs. Linton Heathcliff, had she and I struck up an attachment, as her good nurse desired, and migrated together into the stirring atmosphere of the town!''' (ch. 31).

Lockwood's exit from the scene necessitates yet another flashback. For during the nine months that have elapsed between his trip to London's "stirring atmosphere" and his accidental return to the neighbourhood in September of 1802 a new development has been under way. Thus it devolves on Nelly Dean once more to recapitulate what has happened during Lockwood's absence. His memory of his earlier residence in the area, he admits, had "already grown dim and dreamy" (ch. 32), but there is nothing hazy about the completion of the "Earnshaw Chronicle" which Nelly proudly unfolds for Lockwood. The very concreteness of Cathy's and Hareton's bliss, witnessed by Lockwood himself, compels him "to escape them again." The "fairy tale" he rejected seems perfectly realizable in an ordinary and time-bound world. But the final installment of Nelly's narrative (chs. 32–34) also reminds us of Heathcliff's self-willed escape from temporal bondage. The testimonial of the little shepherd boy who saw Heathcliff and "a woman, yonder," roaming the moors (ch. 34), reintroduces an order of reality not governed by the regularity of clocks. Lockwood's concluding attempts to find reassurance in the natural fluctuations of the seasons seem insufficient to allay our belief in Heathcliff's and Catherine's freedom of movement in a dimension outside time. The satisfying – and self-satisfied – conclusions with which the novel's two chief narrators have tried to tie up its temporal strands remain at odds with a reunion of "unquiet" selves liberated at last from the pressures of chronology and history.

The order of telling

Although we must depend largely on the linear narratives of Nelly Dean and Lockwood for the resolution of the "Earnshaw Chronicle," Emily Brontë relies on voices other than theirs for the counter-narrative of Heathcliff's interactions with Catherine. These voices are only partly filtered. Thus, in the first of these important segments, Catherine's voice speaks to us unencumbered in the diary fragment Lockwood reproduces in chapter 3. And in the last of the segments, in chapter 29, Heathcliff's abrupt confession of having violated Catherine's grave on "the day she was buried" (ch. 29) is even freer of Nelly's censorship than Catherine's own memorable confessional, in chapter 9, about the nature of her unchanging love for Heathcliff.

In the speech Nelly dubs as "nonsense" and "folly," Catherine insists on the timelessness of her relation to one who "is more myself than I am" (ch. 9). Whereas her relation to Edgar Linton belongs to the history chronicled by Nelly, Catherine's oneness with Heathcliff, she suggests, belongs to an altogether different order of reality:

My love for Linton is like the foliage in the woods. Time will change it, I'm well aware, as winter changes the trees. My love for Heathcliff resembles the eternal rocks beneath – a source of little visible delight, but necessary. Nelly, I *am* Heathcliff – he's always, always in my mind – not as a pleasure, any more than I am always a pleasure to myself – but as my own being – so, don't talk of our separation again – it is impracticable; and –   (ch. 9)

This interrupted speech, like Heathcliff's own speech in chapter 29, is more like the utterance of a credo. Catherine tries to explain that her "necessary" oneness with Heathcliff has little to do with the sexual "pleasure" that Hindley has felt in Frances's presence, or that later will draw Isabella to Heathcliff. Yet in trying to justify herself to Nelly, Catherine also seems aware that her words will go misunderstood. A similar attitude is adopted by Heathcliff in his own efforts to articulate his monomaniacal pursuit of the disembodied ghost of Catherine. Each speaker only nominally addresses their common interlocutor, Nelly. Maintaining an uncharacteristic "silence" during Heathcliff's monologue in chapter 29, Nelly even admits that he had "only half addressed me" (ch. 29). In each case, it would seem that the reader, rather than Nelly, is intended to be the prime auditor. We must fit these and

Date	Speaker	Subject-matter	Chapter
(a) November 1777 [November 1801]	Catherine	records account of her revolt with Heathcliff in her diary [which is read by Lockwood]	3
(b) November 1777	Heathcliff	reports separation from injured Catherine he left at the Grange	6
(c) Summer 1780	Catherine	tries to define her competing loves for Edgar and Heathcliff	9
(d) January 1784	Catherine	wishes to be a girl again	12
(e) March, 1784	Isabella	writes to Nelly from the Heights	13
(f) March 1784	Isabella	reports flight from Heathcliff after his frenzy upon Catherine's death	17
(g) November 1800	Cathy	admits meeting Linton Heathcliff at the Heights	24
(h) September 1801	Heathcliff	links earlier exhumation of Catherine's grave in 1784 to his recent uncovering of her coffin	29

similar segments into a sequence that eludes Nelly's control, a sequence which confirms the timelessness stressed by Catherine and Heathcliff in their monologic credos, and which therefore begins and ends with segments wrenched out of chronological order. We first hear the words of a long-dead child before Lockwood can grasp their full import. And we last hear Heathcliff reporting in 1801 of his violation of the long-dead Catherine's grave on her burial day in March 1784. Time itself is deliberately being violated.

The sequence that begins with Catherine's diary entry and ends with Heathcliff's account of his grave-tampering dwells on the compulsive union-through-separation of their twin selves. It is made up of eight major segments and it relies on the voices of four separate narrators, as shown in the table on the previous page.

There are significant links among these fragments. Although the first, (a), and the last, (h), seem to be farthest apart, they are also closest to each other in time: Lockwood's reading of Catherine's diary and his subsequent dreams occur just two months after Heathcliff's enunciation of his "strong faith in ghosts" who remain unfettered by time and space (ch. 29). Again, even though Heathcliff's speech comes almost eighteen years after Isabella fled the Heights, he returns in (h) to events we had previously encountered in her narrative in (f). A different sort of temporal superimposition takes place in (g): in trying to describe her attraction to Heathcliff's son through metaphors borrowed from nature, Cathy unwittingly recapitulates portions of the speech her mother made twenty years before in (c) when Catherine tried to distinguish her love for the two men whose names have been telescoped into that of Linton Heathcliff. The repeated references to storms, sleet, and snow that punctuate segments (a), (b), (c), (d), (f), and (h) help to establish a rhythm that further connects these segments and lifts them out of the linear narratives of Nelly and Lockwood. There are more such connections, but, lacking the space to consider each of these eight units, I shall concentrate on the first and last only, and stress their links to each other and to some of the intervening fragments.

Emily Brontë makes sure that the defiant voice of the still "unknown Catherine" should be heard by Lockwood and the reader well before she introduces that of the "steady, reasonable" Mrs. Dean who can accommodate herself to the many "masters" she tries to serve (chs. 3, 7). We share Lockwood's sympathy for the rebel child who defies Joseph's authority on a rainy Sunday afternoon; Catherine's own closeness to her fellow-rebel Heathcliff thus draws us into a quadruple alliance: Catherine, Heathcliff, Lockwood, and the reader are briefly at one. The scene Catherine describes confirms this sense of fusion. She informs us that she and Heathcliff have hidden from Joseph by fastening "our pinafores together" and hanging them up as "a curtain" to ward off adult intrusion (ch. 3). The detail carries an emblematic significance that contemporary readers would well have understood. Girl and boy are identically attired because they are at that pre-pubescent stage which late eighteenth-century and nineteenth-century culture chose to treat as sexually undifferentiated. In Coleridge's famous poem about the reconciliation of contraries, "Frost at Midnight," the speaker nostalgically remembers the androgynous phase in which he and a "sister more beloved" than any other kinsman were still "both clothed alike" (lines 42, 43). By placing his sleeping infant son Hartley (on whom Branwell Brontë later tried to press his own writings) in a natural scene in which seasonal change can be abolished, the speaker imaginatively recovers the Edenic fusions that he has lost.

Emily Brontë also stresses the fragility of the fusion Catherine and Heathcliff try to maintain. Joseph tears down the curtain of interwined pinafores almost as soon as it has been hung up. But another female attire will protect the boy and girl and allow them to roam in a landscape much like that into which Coleridge places Hartley, freed from the temporal burdens that weigh down his father. The girl who begins her diary by wishing that "my father were back again" records Heathcliff's "pleasant suggestion" that "we should appropriate the dairy woman's cloak, and have a scamper on the moors, under its shelter" (ch. 3). In Coleridge's poem, a vernal paradise can be superimposed on a wintry world of frost when the male speaker assumes the cloak of chief nurturer of his "dear Babe." In Brontë's novel, the "flooding" rain Catherine describes (ch. 3) and the "suffocating" snow that drove Lockwood into her bedroom (ch. 2) can be annulled by a maternal shield that protects the two parentless children who are convinced that they "cannot be damper, or colder, in the rain" than they are indoors (ch. 3). The fusion which Coleridge reinstates at the end of his poem will be more difficult to maintain in *Wuthering Heights*. Brontë deliberately evokes, yet undercuts, this Romantic precedent later in this sequence when she has Catherine mock the "sweetly" sleeping baby Hareton during her confession in chapter 9 and has Isabella demand the removal of the wailing baby Cathy as she recounts the circumstances of her flight from Heathcliff in chapter 17 (segments [b] and [f], in the table above).

Heathcliff's insistence, in chapter 29, that Catherine's elusive "spirit" remains with him as much as ever is marked by the same defiance she displayed as a child and as a sexual adult. Heathcliff's most recent expedition to Catherine's coffin becomes almost indistinguishable, in his telling, from his vivid recollection of his original pilgrimage to her freshly dug grave on a snowy day in March of 1784. On his latest grave-tampering, Heathcliff is surprised to hear from the sexton that if fresh air were to blow on the dead woman's face her features "would change" (ch. 29). To him, those features have remained unaltered after nearly eighteen years of entombment. Past and present are identical. If the sexual differences distinguishing a female and male child were erased in Catherine's 1777 diary entry, the differences between a female corpse and a living male body are of little consequence to the man whose continued belief in Catherine's "presence" leads him to the hope of "dissolving with her" (ch. 29).

Heathcliff's delayed account of his possession by Catherine on the day of her burial takes us back to the deposition given, at the time, by Isabella, back in chapter 17. Only now, a dozen chapters later, do the outward actions that seemed so frenzied and demoniacal to Isabella become more intelligible. Conscious only of the indignities that Heathcliff heaped on her and Hindley when they vainly tried to bar him from the Heights, Isabella was unaware of his desperate need to enter. Heathcliff, we are now allowed to see, was frantically pursuing the ghost he "could *almost* see" at the cemetery back into Catherine's old room (ch. 29). Heathcliff's "expression of unspeakable sadness" had struck Isabella the morning after his return: his eyes seemed wet with weeping, she observed, and his lips were devoid of their usual sneer. But eager to hurt him at a moment of "weakness," Isabella was not disposed to sympathize with his unexplained grief. Heathcliff's later narrative, however, permits us to provide that sympathy. We can even understand why Isabella's taunts should have had the intended effect of a "dart." She assures Heathcliff that had he married Catherine he would only have encountered the same "detestation and disgust" she feels for him. Isabella is wounded by the knife the enraged Heathcliff hurls at her, but the wound she has inflicted on him is deeper than she will ever know.

Heathcliff's belated report of his search for the dead Catherine also helps to explain the melodramatic behavior Lockwood observed in chapter 3 after he informed Heathcliff of the ghost's appearance. At first, Lockwood attributed Heathcliff's "agitation," his teeth-grindings and nail-crushings to sheer "cowardice" (ch. 3). When his strained humourous allusions to "that minx, Catherine Linton, or Earnshaw," are cut short by Heathcliff's "savage vehemence," Lockwood must revise his diagnosis. Still, though aware of the genuine grief that accompanied Heathcliff's physical outbursts and "uncontrollable passion of tears," Lockwood prefers to dismiss such actions as incomprehensible "folly," the same word Nelly uses to question Catherine's assumption that she can retain Heathcliff while marrying Edgar. Nelly's guardedness is rooted in prudence; Lockwood's defensiveness, however, stems from his fear of any excessive display of emotions.

But the excessiveness seems appropriate to the reader after we have become privy to the pathos of Heathcliff's visitations, "through eighteen years," of the bedchamber he regards as an enchanted space (ch. 3). Lockwood was haunted by the "glare of white letters" that made the darkness swarm with Catherines "as vivid as spectres" (ch. 3). Heathcliff has pursued the "specter of a hope" in the same vicinity:

> When I went from home, I hastened to return; she *must* be somewhere at the Heights, I was certain! And when I slept in her chamber − I was beaten out of that − I couldn't lie there; for the moment I closed my eyes, she was either outside the window, or sliding back the panels, or entering the room, or even resting her darling head on the same pillow she did when a child. And I must open my lids to see. And so I opened and closed them a hundred times a night − to be always disappointed! It racked me! I have often groaned aloud . . .   (ch. 29)

Sympathy for Heathcliff as well as for Catherine is achieved through the sequence that culminates in this eighth segment. The agony suffered by the man whom Lockwood saw "suppressing a groan" becomes more accessible than before. Catherine's appearance to Lockwood rather than to the playmate who so intensely wants a restoration of their former oneness confirms Heathcliff's complaint that he has become "the sport of . . . unbearable torture" (ch. 29). If Nelly's narrative makes us welcome the happy ending of the "Earnshaw Chronicle," the sequence that begins with a childhood romp on the moors asks us to endorse Heathcliff's irrational wish for reincorporation with the ghost of his childhood. The reunion of Catherine and Heathcliff may not be as pleasurable as that of Hareton and Cathy. But, to adapt Catherine's own words, it is a necessity. Like Heathcliff himself, the reader cannot rest until the separation of kindred souls has been overcome.

Location and dislocation

Wuthering Heights is one of the most kinetic of English novels. Its characters are in constant motion. From Lockwood's two trips to the Heights in the opening chapters to Cathy's and Hareton's projected return to the Grange at the end, the traffic between the novel's two primary settings establishes rhythms that are crucial to its meanings. Just as our progress through a musical composition or a poem is influenced by the alternations between stronger and softer strains, so are we affected by the movement between the frenzy of the Heights and the more moderate pace of life at the Grange. After we have observed a demented Hindley try to cram a knife down Nelly's throat and drop little Hareton "over the banister" (ch. 9), or seen Heathcliff batter Hindley into submission (ch. 17), Lockwood's own unexpectedly violent action of rubbing "to and fro" the wrist of his ghostly invader (ch. 3) strikes us, in retrospect, as typical behavior for a sojourner at the Heights. Conversely, the haven offered by the more cultured Grange, with its well-stocked library and fruitful orchards, we discover, rightly appeals to other refugees besides the overwrought Lockwood.

Nelly's own ambulations between Wuthering Heights and Thrushcross Grange help to mark off the major shifts in action. As noted before, though raised at the Heights, as Heathcliff and the Earnshaw children were, Nelly identifies far more strongly with the sedate and civilized ways of the Grange. Of her many "masters," Edgar Linton is by far her favourite. Still, despite the final movement to the home of the Lintons, the titular dwelling named after the "atmospheric tumult" caused by the north wind acts as the novel's prime magnet. Wuthering Heights first draws Heathcliff and Frances from the outer world. Once taken over by Heathcliff, it attracts Isabella, Cathy, and, of course, the curious Lockwood, all whom will become disenchanted with the energies they at first found so compelling.

Catherine Earnshaw's attraction to the refinements of the Grange and to Edgar Linton's softer male beauty thus runs contrary to the direction taken by most of the other characters. The boy Heathcliff, through whose narrative we get a fuller picture of Thrushcross Grange than we ever obtain from Lockwood, is baffled by Catherine's willingness to remain there after her wounding by the dog Skulker. Although he is as awed as she is by the "splendid place carpeted with crimson," he shrewdly perceives that the civilized Linton veneer merely disguises a brutality which the primitive Earnshaws openly acknowledge. The "good children" he satirizes so mercilessly fight over a lapdog they threaten to tear apart; their father, who will lecture Hindley for neglecting Catherine's upbringing, abuses his power as a magistrate when he vows to hang Heathcliff on the spot, "before he shows his nature in his acts" (ch. 6). As he observes Catherine from without, Heathcliff is surprised by her failure to defy an authority as hypocritical as Joseph's had been. He expects to be beckoned as a rescuer once again: "if Catherine had wished to return, I intended shattering their great glass panes to a million fragments, unless they let her go" (ch. 6).

Instead, Catherine anticipates her later choice of Grange over Heights. Heathcliff notices how she sits "on the sofa quietly" and allows herself to be tamed by the same prudish "dame" who had "placed her spectacles on her nose and raised her hands in horror" on inspecting the alien "gipsy" boy. Catherine even permits this genteel mother-figure to remove the cloak she had shared with Heathcliff:

Mrs. Linton took off the grey cloak of the dairy maid which we had borrowed for our excursion, shaking her head, and expostulating with her, I suppose; she was a young lady and they made a distinction between her treatment and mine. Then the woman servant brought a basin of warm water, and washed her feet; and Mr. Linton mixed a tumbler of negus, and Isabella emptied a plateful of cakes into her lap, and Edgar stood gaping at a distance. Afterwards, they dried and combed her beautiful hair, and gave her a pair of enormous slippers, and wheeled her to the fire, and I left her, as merry as she could be, dividing her food between the little dog and Skulker whose nose she pinched as he ate . . .   (ch. 6)

Catherine's domestication and enculturation have begun. Even the mastiff whose mouth had dripped "bloody slaver" now feeds as daintily as Fanny the lapdog.

Heathcliff's observation, from his "station as a spy" of Catherine's submission to the ways of the Grange resembles that of the Frankenstein Monster who also looks from without at the domesticity denied to him. His exclusion from the acts of attention Catherine welcomes will eventually lead to Heathcliff's sadism and cause him to be branded as "demon" and "monster" by those who fail to understand the sources of his rage. But Heathcliff also differs from Shelley's creature. Whereas the lonely and misshapen creature desperately wants to be integrated with an Other it might claim as friend or kin, Heathcliff has already fully enjoyed the companionship which his counterpart can never find. His sense of betrayal, therefore, is all the more acute. How can the incipient young lady he watches from his outsider's "station" be so "merry" in the very act of forgetting her playmate? Her seeming readiness to accept her separation from him will rankle and deepen. This scene — like the later one in which Heathcliff fails to hear the second half of Catherine's confession to Nelly — provides the rationale for the shape of his later revenge. Unlike the Frankenstein Monster who burns houses and tears apart the relations denied to him, Heathcliff will want to possess both of the houses from which he has been barred as a replacement for the space vacated by Catherine.

And yet, as both Catherine and Heathcliff will discover, neither Heights nor Grange is a location fit to contain their unquiet spirits. As each of them gradually comes to realize, they belong instead to an in-between world of thresholds or limina. In "Dark 'Otherness' in *Wuthering Heights*," a chapter in her *The English Novel: Form and Function* (1953), Dorothy Van Ghent discussed the recurrent role that windows and doors play in a book which searches for a domain that might mediate between the "inside" and the "outside." When, two months before her death, the delirious Catherine wishes she "were out of doors . . . a girl again, half savage, and hardy, and free," she opens the window, "careless of the frosty air," and calls out across the moors, beckoning Heathcliff to find his way to her (ch. 12). Though Nelly and Edgar quickly shut the window, Catherine knows that she can no longer be contained at the Grange, where she will die, or the Kirkyard, where she will be buried, or even the Heights, where she will haunt Heathcliff. To move from the "threshold of hell" to "within sight of my heaven," Heathcliff eventually seeks Catherine beyond the walls of any human enclosure (ch. 34). Found gazing intently at "something within two yards distance" by Nelly, the starving Heathcliff at last narrows the gap that separates him from the space he covets. When Nelly comes upon his corpse in Catherine's old bedroom, she remarks that the soldered window has now swung open and that the "face and throat were washed with rain," in a final act of ablution (ch. 34).

Both Catherine and Heathcliff come to regard their own bodies as an obstacle that bars them from reaching the liminal space where they expect to merge. When Catherine says, "I'm tired, tired of being enclosed here" (ch. 15), she is not just referring to her room at the Grange, but also to the "shattered prison" her body has become. Lockwood may choose to confine the dead to their tombs in the graveyard of Gimmerton Kirk, placed at the crossroads between the Heights and the Grange. But we nonetheless retain a contrary sense of their continued mobility. Catherine has vowed that she will "not lie there by myself" (ch. 12), and Heathcliff has made sure to leave the side of the coffin nearest to his own loose (ch. 29). The testimony of the shepherd boy and Joseph's claim that he has seen the two wanderers "on every rainy night" from his window at the Heights seem to confirm Heathcliff's own belief in the activity of ghosts. Even Nelly, who admits her fear of "being out in the dark, now," eagerly awaits the shift to the Grange (ch. 34). As the locale of their first separation, Thrushcross Grange is unlikely to be visited by the reunited pair.

The rhythms of repetition

Repetition is an integral part of several of the structural devices we have so far examined in this chapter. The recurrent traffic between the Heights and the Grange, the returns to Catherine's oak-panelled bed, the storms that punctuate major comings and goings help to pattern *Wuthering Heights*. Iteration contributes to an increasing sense of familiarity: as disoriented at first as Lockwood, we welcome the emergence of sign-posts for the bearings that we had found difficult to discern. We become habituated to un-expected rhythms by the periodic appearance of images that may originally have struck us as arbitrary or eccentric: the opening and closing of gates and windows and doors; the aggression and pacification of eight individualized dogs; the reading and rejection of books; the consumption and rejec-tion of food (notably porridge); the confinement of the characters into locked enclosures and the rambling across open fields and wind-swept moors.

As the novel's main keeper of order and periodicity, Nelly tries to control its flow. She is in charge of replications – literally so, when she takes over the roles of both Frances and Catherine by converting each woman's child into her own "bonny little nursling" (ch. 8); and culturally so, when she resolutely opposes anything that strikes her as anomalous or unprecedented. Like any traditionalist, Nelly relies on proven antecedents. She finds these either in her own direct observa-tion of the predictabilities of life – "one set of faces, and one series of actions, from year's end to year's end" – or in the shared wisdom she extracts from Edgar Linton's library, where she proudly claims to have sifted every single book (ch. 7). Departures from the norm, on the other hand, are always unsettling to Nelly. The extraordinary and the unique – the strange boy Heathcliff; the difficulties Catherine meets when she tries to articulate feelings for which she can find no ready-made expression; dreams, delirium, and even Nelly's own atypical sickness and convalescence (which Cathy is quick to exploit) – inevitably evoke her suspicion and distrust. Her sickness discomforts Nelly precisely because it is unparalleled, "a calamity never before experienced prior to that period, and never, I am thankful to say, since" (ch. 23). When Heathcliff in-forms her that he feels "a strange change approaching," she immediately picks up on the word she finds most troublesome: "'But what do you mean by a *change*, Mr. Heathcliff?' I said, alarmed at his manner" (ch. 33). Though hardly as rigid and undeviating as Joseph, Nelly nonetheless prefers to accommodate herself to established patterns of recurrence. It is no coincidence that she should prefer the conventional Edgar Linton to her three unpredictable and volatile "masters" at the Heights.

Yet Emily Brontë does not only use repetition as a means to subdue the unusual, for she also enlists it, quite to the contrary, to unfix the certainties on which Nelly depends. Repeatedly, characters are startled by resemblances, similarities of appearance which can lead to scenes of misrecognition and, in consequence, to a questioning and even an undermining of fixed identity. In these dramas of misrecognition characters become substitutes for one another. Significantly enough, Brontë forces one such startling mistake on Nelly herself when she places her, not within the confines of either Grange or Heights, but rather in one of those intermediary liminal spaces of blending more characteristically associated in the novel with Heathcliff and Catherine. Nelly leaves the protection of the Grange on "a bright, frosty afternoon" in the opening of chapter 11, yet becomes arrested as she goes "out of my way" towards the village of Gimmerton:

I came to a stone where the highway branches off on to the moor at your left hand; a rough sand-pillar, with the letters W. H. cut on its north side, on the east, G., and on the south-west, T. G. It serves as a guide-post to the Grange, and Heights, and village.

The sun shone yellow on its grey head, reminding me of summer; and I cannot say why, but all at once, a gush of child's sensations flowed into my heart. Hindley and I held it a favourite spot twenty years before.

I gazed long at the weather-worn block; and, stooping down, perceived a hole near the bottom still full of snail-shells and pebbles, which we were fond of storing there with more perishable things; and, as fresh as reality, it appeared that I beheld my early playmate seated on the withered turf, his dark, square head bent forward, and his little hand scooping out the earth with a piece of slate.

"Poor Hindley!" I exclaimed, involuntarily.

I started – my bodily eye was cheated into a momentary belief that the child lifted its face and stared straight into mine! It vanished in a twinkling; but, immediately, I felt an irresistible yearning to be at the Heights. Superstition urged me to comply with this impulse. Supposing he should be dead! I thought – or should die soon – supposing it were a sign of death!   (ch. 11)

Nelly assumes that the boy who appears and vanishes before her is the ghost of her childhood companion, Hindley. She is, after all, in a state of receptivity similar to that in which Lockwood found himself when visited by a phantom child. Despite the marker that clearly sets off distinct and separate localities, Nelly has imposed summer on winter frosts, childhood reminiscences of a shared past on the lonely reality of her adult present. Her yearning to be at the Heights and her sudden fear for the fate of her former playmate anticipate the delirious Catherine's own nostalgia, in the very next chapter, for childhood at "the Heights, and every early association, and my all in all, as Heathcliff was at that time" (ch. 12). Both passages are suffused with echoes from Wordsworth's own poetry of revisitation to the lost Edens of childhood: "Tintern Abbey," "Strange Fits of Passion Have I Known," and "Lucy Gray."

But the ghost-child Nelly assumes to be a figment of her imagination turns out to be quite real. Her "bodily eye" has not been "cheated," after all. As Nelly rushes back to the Heights, trembling for "poor Hindley," she is greeted by the same "apparition" she met before; the "brown-eyed boy" waiting for her has merely "outstripped" her. And he is Hareton, "*my* Hareton," she now recognizes, and not Hindley. Lest she retain any lingering doubts about the solidity of this presumed ghost of childhood past, the boy greets her by throwing a rock that hits her bonnet and by unloading "a string of curses" he has learned from Heathcliff. The figure for whom Nelly mistook Hareton is as much his antagonist as Heathcliff's. Hindley, whom the boy calls "Devil Daddy" cannot "bide me," Hareton tells Nelly, "because I swear at him" (ch. 11).

The confusion makes a shambles of Nelly's clinging to precedent. Although Hareton looks close enough to Hindley to be mistaken by her for a reincarnation of his natural father, he acknowledges Heathcliff as his primary model: "he pays Dad back for what he gies to me − he curses Dad for cursing me − he says I mun do as I will" (ch. 11). Heathcliff is using Hareton to replicate his own childhood deprivation under Hindley, who, in turn, was avenging his own father's preference of the adopted stranger to his legitimate son. One set of repetitions vies with another. The orderly succession in which Edgar Linton believes – and which Nelly hopes to uphold – is countered by a cycle that merely iterates the anarchy of the Heights.

Other such confusions establish likenesses at spots unexpected by the reader or undesired by the characters. When the newly-wed Isabella is "so vexed" by her degradation at the Heights that she throws her supper-tray on the floor and weeps in anger and frustration, Joseph mistakes her for that other rebel, Catherine: "Weel done, Miss Cathy! Weel done, Miss Cathy!," he derisively screeches, "Hahsiver, t'maister sall just tum'le o'er them brocken pots, un' then we's hear summut" (ch. 13). To Joseph, all female antagonists are one and the same. Just as he is willing to identify with whoever male "maister" is in power at the Heights without any sense of contradiction whatsoever, so does he regard Isabella and Catherine, or Catherine and Cathy, as interchangeable. But his misapprehension does more than underscore his rigidity. It also confirms what Brontë allowed Heathcliff to discern much earlier when he observed the anarchic behaviour of the "good" children at the Grange: beneath their civilized veneer lurk forces that can be as aggressive as those which the Earnshaws display. Hence, the newly arrived Isabella longingly fingers the "curiously constructed pistol" with a knife on its barrel that Hindley displays; she allows that "a hideous notion struck me: How powerful I should be possessing such an instrument!" (ch. 13). Nor is she allowed to forget that the Grange from which she comes had its own instruments of violence. After picking up the pots she has "brocken," Isabella suddenly recognizes Throttler, the fierce dog Hareton had tried to unleash, "as a son of our old Skulker" (the mastiff that had bitten Catherine). She remembers that "it had spent its whelphood at the Grange, and was given by my father to Mr. Hindley" (ch. 13).

Genealogy itself, then, can produce something other than straightforward recapitulations. Not only dogs, but children, betray unexpected affinities with those who belong to an earlier generation. To Nelly, Hareton may look like Hindley, but since Isabella is struck by the resemblance between Hindley's eyes and those of a "ghostly Catherine's, with all their beauty annihilated," she also detects in Hindley's son a "look of Catherine's in his eyes and about his mouth" (ch. 13). Those Hindley–Catherine eyes also connect the cousins Cathy and Hareton to each other. When Heathcliff confronts the insubordination of the younger pair, he is angered by the young woman's "infernal eyes" whose accusatory stare reminds him of her mother's. But it is the couple's joint resemblance to Catherine which disarms him, as Nelly explains to Lockwood:

> They lifted their eyes together, to encounter Mr. Heathcliff. Perhaps you have never remarked that their eyes are precisely similar, and they are those of Catherine Earnshaw. The present Catherine has no other likeness to her except a breadth of forehead, and a certain arch of nostril that makes her appear rather haughty, whether she will or not. With Hareton the resemblance is carried farther; it is singular at all times.   (ch. 33)

In a novel in which the duplication of the names "Catherine" and the existence of two "Heathcliffs" and of three male characters whose first name begins with the letter "H" cause considerable confusion, "resemblance" seems indeed to be "carried farther" than usual. Cathy Linton and Linton Heathcliff, that other cousin-pair, find two balls "among a heap of old toys" at the Heights. As Cathy recounts it: "One was marked C., and the other H.; I wished to have the C., because that stood for Catherine, and the H. might be for Heathcliff, his name; but the bran came out of H., and Linton didn't like it" (ch. 24). Cathy is sure that the ball marked "C." belonged to her mother; but she cannot be as positive about the other ball, which probably was not Heathcliff's – Linton Heathcliff's father – but Hindley's, the father of Hareton. The stuffing that spills out of the "H." ball makes it useless for play, just as the playmate Cathy has chosen will turn out to be useless as a husband. But Cathy can find a better "H." mate in Hareton. For he, after all, is the son of Hindley as well as the heir of Heathcliff, who feels closer to Hareton than to Linton Heathcliff, his own offspring.

Heathcliff, too, is struck by Hareton's "startling likeness to Catherine," after the young man who has shed all marks of his former rustication sides with Cathy (ch. 33). But Heathcliff has lost interest in the "material appearance" of the cousin-lovers. He prefers to regard Hareton as "a personification of my youth, not a human being." On the verge of leaving all physical attachments behind him, Heathcliff makes Hareton the incarnation of "the ghost of my immortal love, of my wild endeavours to hold my right" (ch. 33). He cedes all rights to the one who becomes his sole mourner. Catherine had regarded Heathcliff as being more herself than she was. Heathcliff now seems to regard the son of Hindley, who looks more like Catherine than Catherine's daughter does, as an emblem of fusions that could not be obtained in a material world. Hareton regains the Heights lost by his father yet follows the path Catherine had taken when she moved from the Heights to the Grange. He becomes the repository of the novel's many repetitions. He is the dead Catherine's nephew, her son-in-law, her look-alike. He is also the son she was not allowed to bear to either of his two fathers, Hindley and Heathcliff, the competing claimants to the ball marked "H." and to the building marked "H.," the Heights. We are now ready to interpret the competitions on which *Wuthering Heights* is based.

Chapter 3

The meanings of
Wuthering Heights

The dialectics of power

Emily Brontë asks us to attend to the words of the child Catherine before she introduces Nelly and Heathcliff as the two figures who will wrangle over her later utterances. And she forces Lockwood to respond to the *ur*-text of Catherine's diary before she presents the adult Catherine's statements to Nelly and Heathcliff. Catherine thus acts as the prime purveyor of Brontë's myth of a sexual fall from a prepubescent childhood Eden, a myth which the other three characters help to interpret through their divergent reactions.

In this sense, Catherine Earnshaw can be said to act as the novel's tentative ideologue. She is rejected by Lockwood as a ghost-child and by Nelly as soon as she becomes "the queen of the country-side" (ch. 8). Nelly admits that "I own I did not like her after her infancy was past; and I vexed her frequently by trying to bring down her arrogance" (ch. 8). But Heathcliff, who hears only the first half of Catherine's speech to Nelly in chapter 9, resents Catherine's rise to power for different reasons. Nelly begrudges the ease with which Catherine can "escape from a disorderly, comfortless home into a wealthy, respectable one" and become "wife of young Linton." Heathcliff, however, sees Catherine's move to the Grange and marriage to Edgar as a betrayal of their childhood oneness. He does not know that Catherine still considers herself to be united to him, and that she hopes that her move might enable her to "place him out of my brother's power" (ch. 9).

Instead, Heathcliff furiously follows Catherine's precedent. He too will enlist his early Earnshaw connections and his sexual appeal in his own rise to social pre-eminence. If, as a child, Catherine had been his ally against the adult powers wielded by Hindley and Joseph, she now fuels his drive to gain ascendancy in the world of power. Strife and competition mark all of Heathcliff's interactions with Catherine after his return. Angry at her for having overwhelmed Edgar by her beauty, Heathcliff revenges himself by seducing Edgar's sister. Even the farewell scene between the two lovers is remarkable for the antagonism with which they express the depth of their love. Catherine blames Heathcliff for her impending death with "wild vindictiveness"; he imputes his past, present, and future agonies to her "infernal selfishness" (ch. 15). His grip is so fierce that "blue impressions" are left on her "colourless skin" (ch. 15).

After Catherine's death, Heathcliff collides with his major competitor, Nelly Dean, now as hostile to him as she had been to Catherine before. Although ostensibly fighting over the grandchildren of the man who had brought both Heathcliff and Nelly to the Heights, they actually vie over Catherine's beliefs. Nelly had scoffed at Catherine's allegiance to conflicting orders of reality. Not only had she foreseen that an adherence to a world of power could not be reconciled with the loyalty to an Edenic oneness that Catherine also wanted to maintain, but she had also rejected the latter as a metaphysical chimera. Catherine had asked: "What were the use of my creation if I were entirely contained here?" (ch. 9). For Nelly, however, despite her pieties about an afterlife, earthly containers alone matter.

Unlike Nelly, Heathcliff wants to retain Catherine's belief in their continued oneness. Despite his own materialism, he cannot accept his separation from the dead woman he has tried to disinter. His insatiable hunger for domination stems from his constant need to be compensated for what he has lost. When he refuses Nelly's plea that the dispossessed Cathy be allowed to live at the Grange under her supervision, Heathcliff adduces his desire to rent the estate to a tenant. But his interest is not really monetary, as his sarcastic afterthought reveals: "I want my children about me, to be sure —

besides that lass owes me her services for her bread; I'm not going to nurture her in luxury and idleness" (ch. 29). Heathcliff's reference to "my children" is derisive. He loathes the weak son he has fathered. Linton Heathcliff reminds him of Isabella, and hence of the Linton features Catherine had preferred to Heathcliff's own. And Cathy's defiant eyes recall, not her Linton father, but her Earnshaw mother. Only Hareton, on whom he imposes his own conditions of servitude under Hindley, can be considered as Heathcliff's "child."

Whereas Heathcliff savours imposing on the surviving Lintons and Earnshaws the disempowerment he suffered after Hindley's abuse and Catherine's desertion, Nelly wants to extend the power originally granted to her by old Earnshaw, her first "master." Like Catherine before him, Heathcliff finds it increasingly difficult to reconcile participation in a world of power with his steadfast loyalty to a vanished childhood bond. Nelly, on the other hand, shifts from her own allegiance to Hindley to an identification with the interests of Edgar Linton. While Heathcliff exacts "services" from Cathy and Hareton, the children of gentry-folk he has "de-classed," Nelly puts her own serviceableness to good use. As physically healthy as Heathcliff (whose sturdiness as a child she admired), she assures a worried Cathy that her role as a parental surrogate is unlikely to be cut short. Not only has she outlived the two mothers who left their children to be reared by her (just as Maria Brontë delegated the rearing of her young to her Nelly-like sister, Elizabeth Branwell), but she also correctly anticipates that she will outlive Cathy's debilitated father.

Nelly's reassurance of Cathy suggests the extent to which she has come to control the Grange before Edgar Linton's death. Her tone is not that of a menial, but that of someone whose assumption of a motherly role has almost converted her into the wife of the child's "papa":

"Catherine, why are you crying, love?" I asked, approaching and putting my arm over her shoulders. "You mustn't cry because papa has a cold; be thankful it is nothing worse."

She now put no further restraint on her tears; her breath was stifled by sobs.

"Oh, it *will* be something worse," she said. "And what shall I do when papa and you leave me, and I am by myself? I can't forget your words, Ellen, they are always in me. How life will be changed, how dreary the world will be, when papa and you are dead."

"None can tell, whether you won't die before us," I replied. "It's wrong to anticipate evil. We'll hope there are years and years to come before any of us go: master is young, and I am strong, and hardly forty-five. My mother lived till eighty, a canty dame to the last. And suppose Mr. Linton were spared till he saw sixty, that would be more years than you have counted, Miss. And would it not be foolish to mourn a calamity above twenty years beforehand?"

"But Aunt Isabella was younger than papa," she remarked, gazing up with timid hope to seek further consolation.

"Aunt Isabella had not you and me to nurse her," I replied. "She wasn't as happy as master; she hadn't as much to live for. All you need do, is to wait well on your father, and cheer him by letting him see you cheerful; and avoid giving him anxiety on any subject — mind that, Cathy! I'll not disguise but you might kill him, if you were wild and reckless, and cherished a foolish, fanciful affection for the son of a person who would be glad to have him in his grave . . ."   (ch. 22)

Cathy's fear of parental desertion recalls Catherine's own words of desolation in the opening of her diary ("I wish my father were back again"). But Catherine had a playmate in Heathcliff, whereas Cathy is warned not to play with the outsider's son (whom she will nonetheless present with the ball marked "H.") Nelly has ceased to be the outsider she once was. She has assumed the position left vacant by the many wives who predecease their mates in the book (Mrs Earnshaw, Mrs Linton, Frances, Isabella, and Catherine). Her own mother's longevity inspires Nelly with confidence that she might even outlast the fearful child before her. Nelly hardly soothes Cathy by claiming that the girl may well die before her elders. And she proves quite unfeeling by threatening that any act of deviance might kill the father Cathy loves. Her power in intimidating Cathy contrasts with her inability to influence Catherine. Nelly had not wanted to accompany Catherine to the Grange, despite the "munificent wages" offered by Edgar (ch. 9). She adduced her strong attachment to Hareton at the time, but her concurrent remarks about Catherine's ability to "trample us like slaves" also suggested that she wanted to avoid a power-struggle which she could not expect to win. Unlike Cathy, Catherine could not be manipulated through an invocation of "duty" or paternal law. (When old Earnshaw had asked her why she could "not always be a good lass," she shot back, "Why cannot you always be a good man, father?" Nelly, by way of contrast, remembers how old Earnshaw would "call me a cant lass, and slip a shilling into my hand" [chs. 5, 7].)

Nelly's devotion is to those who reward her and to those she can dominate. Although her attachment to Cathy is as sincere as her love for Hareton, her efforts to have the young woman toe the line of a living father's law are hardly unselfish. Nelly's welfare depends on the unencumbered life of the melancholiac whose sorrows as a widower were compounded by the lack of a male heir (ch. 16). The Grange stays secure as long as Edgar is spared anxiety. Nelly considers herself guardian of her second home. It is she who once again tries to repulse Heathcliff when he comes to woo Cathy on behalf of his sickly son. Heathcliff accosts the girl outside the locked gate. Although Nelly is within, she refuses to admit that she is as much an outsider, the appropriator of someone else's nest, as the new master at the Heights. Hers, too, is a "cuckoo's" story.

When Heathcliff asks Cathy to stop "making love in play" and admit that she is seriously breaking his frail son's heart, he relies on the very same rhetorical tactics Nelly had employed (ch. 22). The symmetry is quite striking. If Heathcliff now exaggerates Cathy's potential culpability in causing his son's death, Nelly has exaggerated Cathy's capacity of killing a beloved "papa." The scene dramatizes the power-struggle between these two outsiders, each of whom covets − though for different reasons − the status that had legitimately been Hindley's and Catherine's. From her side of the locked door, Nelly pleads desperately with her young ward, who stands outdoors, fully exposed to Heathcliff's manipulative blandishments: "Miss Cathy, I'll knock the lock off with a stone. You won't believe that vile nonsense. You can feel in yourself, it is impossible that a person should die for the love of a stranger'' (ch. 22). Nelly is appalled by Cathy's credulity: since Heathcliff so blatantly argues for a son he despises, he must be "glaringly" lying.

On the surface, Nelly's accusation seems as justified as her protective stance appears to be well-intentioned. But Heathcliff immediately turns the tables on the "worthy Mrs. Dean." He accuses *her* of "double dealing" as soon as he discovers that his overtures to Cathy have been heard by this meddlesome "eaves-dropper." (The scene thus reverses the crucial episode in which a silent Nelly Dean allowed an "eaves-dropping" young Heathcliff, still as innocent as Cathy now is, to misconstrue Catherine's speech, when she neither detained him nor warned Catherine that her words were being overheard.) Heathcliff's counter-attack exploits Cathy's naiveté. Appealing to something she can feel in herself (as Nelly had put it), he insists that people *can* die of love, contrary to Nelly's assertion. By disputing his solicitude for his son, Heathcliff argues, it is Nelly, and not he, who has been the liar. To clinch his devious argument, he asks Cathy to effect an imaginary transposition: "Just imagine your father in my place and Linton in yours; then think how you would value your careless lover, if he refused to stir a step to comfort you, when your father, himself, entreated him" (ch. 22).

Though specious in its analogizing, the trick proves effective, for it enlists Cathy's emotional sympathies, which Heathcliff shrewdly grasps. If we adopt Nelly's perspective here, Heathcliff is a despicable liar. We know that he does not love his son, that he is merely using Linton Heathcliff as a lure in his relentless campaign to amass all the power once denied to him. Yet, as always, Brontë also invites us to look beyond Nelly's perspective. And she enables us to see that Heathcliff — by counting on a loving daughter's filial bond — is doing something quite similar to what Nelly had earlier done to control a potentially "wild and reckless" child. Both rivals vying over Cathy thus enlist her attachment to Edgar in order to obtain mastery over her actions, and, thereby, to secure power for themselves.

Despite the lies Heathcliff fabricates, there actually *is* an element of "truth" in his emotional appeal to Cathy. Nelly brands as "vile nonsense" the notion that practical strangers should die from unfulfilled love. What she disparages as a fictive "little romance" between the two cousins lacks, as far as she is concerned, any solidity. Nelly is not devoid of emotional depth. Indeed, her often-asserted attachment to Hindley almost seems as intense as Heathcliff's childhood bond with Catherine. When she is told that someone has died at the Heights, she ventures the undisguised hope that it might be Heathcliff, "surely?" Told by the physician that it was her "old friend Hindley," she loses her habitual composure: "I confess this blow was greater to me than the shock of Mrs. Linton's death: ancient associations lingered around my heart; I sat down in the porch and wept as for a blood relation" (ch. 17). Yet Nelly manages to shrug off even such painful losses as a predictable aspect of the world of process she stoically accepts. Heathcliff, on the other hand, no more accepts Catherine's death than he accepted their separation while she was still alive. The elusive ghost he pursues for eighteen years may seem a "stranger" to Lockwood, but she cannot estrange Heathcliff, who remembers that Catherine has died from the intensity of their love. What Nelly correctly dismisses as inapplicable to Linton Heathcliff and Cathy nonetheless becomes valid when applied to Heathcliff. He *will* die – and will want to die – for the love of an unseen being.

Thus, when Heathcliff claims that his son is "going to his death" out of the "grief and disappointment" of unfulfilled desire, he is creating a sardonic and characteristically self-lacerating parody of his own insatiable desire for Cathy's mother. Applied to Cathy and to Linton Heathcliff, his story is a fiction. Applied to Catherine and himself, however, this fiction perfectly captures their own obsession. As one who precipitates Catherine's death, dominates Hindley, mesmerizes Isabella, possesses himself of Hareton and Cathy and of their legacies, outwits Edgar and Nelly, and bullies

Lockwood, Heathcliff certainly is by far the most potent
figure in the book, as Charlotte Brontë noted with alarm in
her "Editor's Preface." But Heathcliff turns the voracity
with which he devoured all others on himself. As he confides
to Nelly in one of their last exchanges, he now yearns for self-
consumption far more intensely than he had lusted for powers
which have suddenly lost their old allure.

Physical health, so greatly prized by Nelly, thus becomes a
liability, rather than an asset, for Heathcliff, who wants to
divest himself of his tenacious hold on life. Nelly notes that
her interlocutor is still "quite strong and healthy" (ch. 33).
And Heathcliff himself, as unaware as she is of the proximity
of his death, still engages in a Nelly-like calculus of his
chances of survival: "With my hard constitution, and
temperate mode of living, and unperilous occupation, I ought
to, and probably *shall* remain above ground, till there is
scarcely a black hair on my head" (ch. 33). But then, in a
reversal that shows how far beyond Nelly's realm of survival
of the fittest he has moved, Heathcliff describes his death-
wish with a vividness that eerily presages Emily Brontë's own
self-consummation a bare twelve months after the publication
of *Wuthering Heights*:

And yet I cannot continue in this condition! I have to remind myself
to breathe − almost to remind my heart to beat! And it is like bend-
ing back a stiff spring; it is by compulsion that I do the slightest
act not prompted by one thought, and by compulsion, that I notice
anything alive, or dead, which is not associated with one universal
idea. I have a single wish, and my whole being and faculties are
yearning to attain it. They have yearned toward it so long, and so
unwaveringly, that I'm convinced it *will* be reached − and *soon* −
because it has devoured my existence. I am swallowed in the anticipation of its fulfilment.   (ch. 33)

Ironically enough, Heathcliff's death grants Nelly an even
greater power than that which she had earlier wielded at the
Grange. Indeed, his death gives her the status of a pseudo-
novelist. If she and Heathcliff are viewed as rival authors in
their attempts to shape the destinies of the survivors of the
"Earnshaw Chronicle," then it is quite obviously Nelly's

script, and not his, which dominates the story's ending. The domestic fiction which this female story-teller dispenses from her adopted position by the fireside of a hearth displaces both Catherine's aborted metaphysical romance and Heathcliff's final fiction of reunited ghosts. Nelly had told Cathy that her aunt Isabella might have lived longer if she could have had "you and me to nurse her." Cathy's foster-mother watches gleefully as Cathy dresses Hareton's self-inflicted wound and supervises his transformation into a suitably genteel husband. As complacent as ever, Nelly notes to Lockwood: "I came to sit with them, after I had done my work, and I felt so soothed and comforted to watch them, that I did not notice how time got on. You know, they both appeared, in a measure, my children: I had long been proud of one, and now, I was sure, the other would be a source of equal satisfaction" (ch. 33). Unlike Heathcliff's earlier reference to "my children," Nelly's is sincere. Still, the note of self-gratulation is inescapable. She has indeed "done my work": having fashioned this pair in her own image, Nelly can bless them and rest contented. She is even delighted to have misfired in one of her earlier attempts at authorship: "You see, Mr. Lockwood," she tells the young man she had intended to play Adam to Cathy's Eve, "it was easy enough to win Mrs. Heathcliff's heart." And then she adds with the superiority of hindsight, "but now, I'm glad you did not try." Her task is done; her position assured: "The crown of all my wishes will be the union of those two; I shall envy no one on their wedding day — there won't be a happier woman than myself in England!" (ch. 32).

Brontë, however, strongly suggests that if there is no one as happy as Nelly among the living, there may nonetheless be one happier upon his own wedding to a ghost. Nelly's final empowerment converts her into something like the "beneficent fairy" whom Lockwood could not find among the inhabitants of the Heights. But her ascendancy comes about only through Heathcliff's entry into an altogether different realm. Observing the lovers whom Nelly has come to regard as her offspring, Heathcliff muses:

It is a poor conclusion, is it not, . . . [an] absurd termination to my violent exertions? I get levers and mattocks to demolish the two houses, and train myself to be capable of working like Hercules, and when everything is ready, and in my power, I find the will to lift a slate off either roof has vanished! My old enemies have not beaten me; now would be the precise time to revenge myself on their representatives: I could do it; and none could hinder me. But where is the use? . . . I have lost the faculty of enjoying their destruction, and I am too idle to destroy for nothing.   (ch. 33)

Heathcliff soon discovers that the faculty of enjoyment he has lost can be amply rekindled. The death-wish he indulges seems exquisitely pleasurable to him. Hareton and Nelly remark his excitation, the "strange joyful glitter in his eyes," his ecstatic shivering, his concentration, his perennial smile. The smile disturbs Nelly: "I'd rather have seen him gnash his teeth than smile so" (ch. 34). Heathcliff behaves like a young lover who is about to attain his goal. "I'm too happy," he tells Nelly in one of his last speeches, "and yet I'm not happy enough. My soul's bliss kills my body, but does not satisfy itself" (ch. 34). He is on the verge of fruition: "I have nearly attained *my* heaven." When Nelly finds the wet corpse by the open window in Catherine's bedroom she is startled by the near-orgasmic expression on the dead man's face: "His eyes met mine so keen and fierce, I started; and then he seemed to smile" (ch. 34). She tries "to close his eyes – to extinguish, if possible, that frightful, life-like gaze of exultation, before any one else beheld it." The woman who will preside over the consummation of Cathy's and Hareton's marriage seems disturbed by the possibility of a very different kind of climax.

Nelly worries that she may be blamed for having helped to bring about Heathcliff's death. The physician cannot diagnose the material causes for the "disorder" that killed him, and so Nelly, noted for her earlier concealments, now chooses to conceal also "the fact of his having swallowed nothing for four days, fearing it might lead to trouble" (ch. 34). What "trouble" does she have in mind? Is she afraid of an investigation that might tarnish her access to power? (Nelly, after all, had previously hoped for Heathcliff's death.) Is she, who reproached the dying man for his "selfish, unchristian life,'' fearful that his death might be construed a suicide? Or does she want that troubling "life-like gaze of exultation'' to remain unexplained? Ever the quietist, Nelly is quick to reassure herself: "I am persuaded he did not abstain on purpose; it was the consequence of his strange illness, not the cause'' (ch. 34).

Nelly's remark does not settle the questions she wants to foreclose. For it only reminds us that Heathcliff has chosen to abstain from participating in an order of reality where power is strictly aligned with causes and effects. He has attempted to return to a different order. The unity that existed between him and Cathy was at its strongest when the two were still powerless children, engaged in defiant activities of play, as the diary entry read by Lockwood corroborates. It was Catherine's unwillingness to linger in such a disempowered state that caused the rupture between her and Heathcliff. Her attraction to the refinements of the Grange and her concurrent realization of her own sexual powers stimulated the young Heathcliff's acute feelings of betrayal and led him to adopt, however reluctantly, the tools of social power he came to master. By forsaking those tools, Heathcliff has pushed back the clock in a return to his earlier condition. Growth, process, maturation – valued by Nelly Dean – are cast aside in a desperate act of return to adolescence, the threshold between childhood and adult life, the liminal state which Heathcliff had passed (and in which Lockwood is still floundering). The "life-like gaze of exultation'' that so unnerves Nelly suggests that Heathcliff has not only consummated his long-postponed union with Cathy but that he has also become reintegrated with an earlier self.

As the antagonist of both Heathcliff and Catherine (and of their merger into a single self), Nelly may represent common sense, a life-wish, adaptability, and both physical and mental health. But it was the realization that her sister's novel tilted in an opposite direction that led Charlotte Brontë in her "Editor's Preface'' to uphold Nelly as "a specimen of true benevolence and homely fidelity'' for the Victorian reader.

Modern criticism has more than redressed the balance,

from James Hafley's excessive attack on Nelly's prevarications ("The Villain of *Wuthering Heights*", 1958) to James Kavanaugh's discussion of Nelly as "an agent of patriarchal law" in his *Emily Brontë* (1985). It is certainly true that Emily Brontë extends to Heathcliff and Catherine the sympathy which a self-protective Nelly prefers "to extinguish." But Nelly is neither the paragon Charlotte Brontë makes her out to be, nor is she the villainess indicted by Hafley. It seems just as productive to regard her, as I have tried to do, as one half of a divided authorial presence that is pitted against the other half, represented in the book as Catherine/Heathcliff. As the most physically robust of Patrick Brontë's surviving three daughters (and also as the one who most strongly identified with her moody father), Emily was herself a potential Nelly Dean. At the same time, however, as the least tractable and most private of the sisters, the most resistant to Aunt Branwell's conventional views of child-rearing, and the one least willing to relinquish the childhood fantasy world all four children had shared, Emily was also very much a Catherine/Heathcliff. Despite her greater physical strength, she died before Anne and Charlotte. And, as already noted, the circumstances of her death strangely mirrored Heathcliff's fictional self-consumption.

Wuthering Heights is shaped by the interpenetration of the opposing states of being which William Blake had labelled (in the 1780s and 1790s in which the novel's events are set), "Innocence" and "Experience." To understand Heathcliff's (and Emily Brontë's) rejection of the realm of adult power bequeathed to Nelly and the children she has prepared for Experience, we must inspect more closely the contrary realm which the novel sets up as a pleasurable alternative and endows with energies of its own. But the explanatory mechanisms of the "Earnshaw Chronicle" seem deficient when applied to a romance of Innocence, in which male and female selves try to recover their lost psychic integration. Whenever Heathcliff and Catherine try to articulate the nature of their bond, they become elliptical and find themselves forced to rely on the indirection of similes, metaphors, and symbols rather than on the denotative language on which Nelly insists. Brontë herself, however, complements Catherine's and Heathcliff's efforts to express what is so difficult for them to define linguistically. Like many a Romantic poet, she relies on the visionary reality that can be represented through dreams. I have referred to Lockwood's two dreams in the preceding pages, but have tried to avoid affixing significance to their content. Since that content holds a key to the clashing realities which *Wuthering Heights* keeps in suspension, we can at last look at both dreams and relate them to Catherine's and Heathcliff's own accounts of the vicissitudes suffered by their desire for each other.

Fantasy/play and sexual maturation

Lockwood's two dreams respond directly to the two entries he has read in Catherine's diary. Still "scrawled in an unformed childish hand," these entries already point to the imminent loss of a childhood Eden which the ensuing chapters then dramatize. The oneness of the child-rebels who defy the adult authority of Joseph and Hindley is about to be splintered. Their unity as an androgynous whole will be replaced by their individuation as sexually distinct adolescents.

Of the two children, Catherine evinces a greater interest in adult sexuality. She observes Frances and Hindley, the newly-weds, with fascination and scorn. Suddenly self-conscious about such erotic behaviour, she remarks their "kissing and talking nonsense by the hour − foolish palaver we should be ashamed of" (ch. 3). More than Heathcliff, Catherine is also drawn to language, whether "palaver" or not. Despite her antipathy to the authority of the Word, contained in the tracts that Joseph tries to foist on her and Heathcliff, she delays an outing with her playmate in order to authorize herself in writing. She endorses his proposal of a scamper on the moors as a "pleasant suggestion" and yet takes the time to write for twenty minutes more. Of the two, she is clearly farther down the road toward socialization.

The first diary entry also suggests that the articles of clothing which have symbolized the union and equality between the two children can offer them a precarious protection at best. The pinafores (an androgynous attire, as noted before) which Catherine fastens as a curtain are readily torn asunder by Joseph, who easily violates the sanctuary she had tried to preserve. Heathcliff's choice of the "dairy woman's cloak" is intended to offer both children a "shelter," not from indoor adult male assailants, but rather from the inclement weather without. It is significant that the cloak should be associated with the working class and with maternal nurture (dairy-milk will replace mother's milk in the later upbringing of both Hareton and Cathy). Both of these associations suggest the boy's resistance to the social identity conferred on children by the middle-class perpetuators of a male lineage. But it is just as significant that Catherine will soon be stripped of this protective cloak by Mrs. Linton at the Grange, where she will adopt the identity of a feminine young lady. As she later tries to rationalize to Nelly, Catherine welcomes the assurances of class and gender because she can "aid Heathcliff to rise" (ch. 9). She insists on her undiminished oneness: "He'll be as much to me as he has been all his lifetime" (ch. 9). But she fails to see that, as the new Mrs Linton, she would become the patroness of her former equal. The fusions of Innocence, as Blake had suggested, cannot be maintained in the contrary state of Experience.

The second and shorter of the diary entries already introduces a foretaste of that alienating perspective. Heathcliff and Catherine are now no longer a "we." Hindley has forbidden the boy to sit with "us" – the socially superior Earnshaws: "he says, he and I must not play together" (ch. 3). The playful defiance that animated the first entry gives way to a style that Lockwood finds "lachrymose." Hindley, victimized earlier by the father who preferred Heathcliff, now exercises the patriarchal prerogative of determining a child's future identity. But Hindley is not only reaffirming class barriers to deny Heathcliff access to the family's estate; he is also trying to prevent a sister on the edge of puberty from consorting with an older boy. Whether correctly or not, Hindley seems to regard a continuation of the alliance between the two children as sexually threatening to his sister's virginity. True to his name, he becomes a hinderer when he bars Heathcliff from the bedroom the children had hitherto used as their refuge from adult pressures. Catherine's shell-like oak bed, a sturdier and more private enveloping structure than the torn pinafores or the dairy woman's easily stripped coat, can no longer be shared by Heathcliff. Yet both Catherine and he desire to recover their union with each other in that lost privileged space. After her exile at the Grange, the delirious Catherine professes to see "my room" and senses that Heathcliff wants her to meet him there (ch. 12). And, as we have seen, Heathcliff expects to find her there after her death; their union as ghosts will be consummated in that bed. But when the spectre at first tries to join Lockwood in her own bed, she so terrifies the virginal young man that he stains their bed-clothes with her blood (ch. 3).

Lockwood's two dreams are as distinct from each other as the two diary entries he has read. Indeed, the first dream constitutes his response to Catherine's first entry, while his more troubled second one picks up the egress from childhood and entry into a gender-differentiated adult reality which the "lachrymose" second entry has recorded. The young man, whose own uneasy mediation between childish behaviour and adult sexuality we have had occasion to note, is "the proper person" to occupy the bed of the two children who had regarded it as a play-space. It is no coincidence that the "child's face" he "obscurely" discerns in the second dream should appear to him rather than to Heathcliff, who so intensely yearns for its return (ch. 3). Heathcliff's assumption of those socio-sexual powers for which Lockwood is still unprepared has led him to betray, as Catherine herself had betrayed, the face of childhood. As we saw in the previous section, only a willed act of retrogression, a shedding of all the adult trappings of power, could restore to Heathcliff the integrated state he shared with Catherine.

Both of Lockwood's dreams are violent. But whereas the

second one unleashes a sexual sadism that takes us by surprise, the first dream's aggressive energies remain comical and playful. These energies resemble those of the first diary entry, which attracted Lockwood when he became "greatly amused to behold an excellent caricature of my friend Joseph, rudely yet powerfully sketched" (ch. 3). Lockwood's first dream replicates Catherine's and Heathcliff's antagonism towards Joseph's religious tracts. The title of one such tract, "Seventy Times Seven, and the First of the Seventy-First: A Pious Discourse delivered by the Reverend Jabes Branderham," catches Lockwood's eye just as as he drowses off and sinks back in bed. In his humorous subversion of a literalist preacher's misreading of Matthew 18, Lockwood becomes, temporarily, a worthy play-fellow of the girl Catherine.

As an Anglican clergyman's daughter, Emily Brontë shows a sure mastery of biblical texts. She allows Lockwood to expose the rigidities of Jabes Branderham's unforgiving theology by injecting ironies that stem from her command of both the Old and New Testaments. Emily, first of all, plays with the fictional preacher's name. The Hebrew name "Jabesh" (which means "dry" and belongs to the father of a murderer and usurper) seems as fitting as "Branderham," given the preacher's dry sermonizing and his eagerness to "brand" others ("her/him") with accusations of sin. More important, however, is Brontë's grasp of the text from which Branderham draws the title of his sermon: Matthew 18. For she makes Branderham misconstrue as an authority for his intolerance some of the most celebrated utterances on charity and fellowship.

Matthew 18, begins with an exposition Branderham significantly omits, namely, the idealization of childhood innocence. Asked to name "the greatest in the kingdom of heaven," Jesus places "a little child" amidst his disciples, and says: "Except ye be converted, and become as little children, ye shall not enter in the kingdom of heaven. . . . And whoso shall receive one such little child in my name receiveth me" (18:1–5). When Peter later demands to know whether forgiveness to an offending "brother" should be extended as far as "seven times," Jesus insists on widening the scope of tolerance far beyond such limits: "I say not unto thee, Until seven times: but, Until seventy times time seven" (18: 21–2). It is this latter portion of Matthew on which Branderham seizes. But he converts Jesus's plea for unlimited tolerance into an attack on four hundred and ninety separate sins he proceeds to enumerate one by one. Lockwood is amazed at the inexhaustible list of offenses, "odd transgressions I had never imagined previously": "Where he searched for them, I cannot tell; he had his private manner of interpreting the phrase, and it seemed necessary the brother should sin different sins on every occasion" (ch. 3).

Significantly enough, Lockwood's behaviour soon resembles that of a squirming boy who has been dragged to chapel by his elders. He is totally bored by the endless catalogue that seems to impress Joseph, who sits next to him in the dream: "Oh, how weary I grew. How I writhed, and yawned, and nodded, and revived! How I pinched, and pricked myself, and rubbed my eyes, and stood up, and sat down again, and nudged Joseph to inform me if he would *ever* have done!" Lockwood's fidgeting, noticed by the preacher who will accuse him of having "gapingly" contorted his "visage" seventy times seven times, is reminiscent of his earlier "winking and making faces" at Juno and her pups, as well as of his covert animosity towards Joseph, who urged Gnasher and Wolf to attack him (chs. 1, 2). Having identified himself with Cathy's attack on Joseph as well as with the child-rebels of the diary, Lockwood at last feels free to take a more active role. Just as Branderham is about to identify the four-hundred-ninety-first sin, Lockwood anticipates him by denouncing the preacher himself "as the sinner of the sin that no Christian need pardon" (ch. 3).

What *is* that unforgivable sin? For Lockwood, the offense is the interminable sermon; inciting the fellow-congregants he addresses as "martyrs" into mounting an open revolt, he urges them to "drag" their leader down from the pulpit, strip him of his authority, and "crush him to atoms." For

Branderham, on the other hand, it is Lockwood's anarchism that is the unpardonable sin. Taking his cue from another biblical text, 2 Samuel 12:7, he points an accusing finger at the young revolutionary and thunders: *"Thou art the Man!"* In the comic row that ensues, Lockwood, "having no weapon to raise in self-defence," grapples with Joseph for possession of a "pilgrim's staff," the old man, but not Lockwood, had brought. Whether or not he gains possession of this emblem of masculine authority remains unclear. What seems certain is that Lockwood somehow remains immune: "blows, aimed at me, fell on other sconces." He thus awakes, intact, aware that the loud rappings that "played Jabes's part" in the dream were caused by a tree-branch rattling against the window (ch. 3).

Despite his own playing a rebel's part, Lockwood's first dream dissolves harmlessly. Yet meanings he has not consciously fathomed will surface in the far more terrifying nightmare that soon follows. These meanings are embedded in the biblical texts with which both Jabes and Lockwood have toyed. Jabes's "Thou art the Man" is spoken by the prophet Nathan in 2 Samuel 12. Like Jesus, Nathan tells a parable which a listener takes literally. Nathan tells King David that a rich sheep-owner slaughtered the single "little ewe lamb" that had been the sole possession of a poor man who had "nourished" her with his children and had treated her "as a daughter" (12:3). Greatly incensed, David vows to mete out the harshest of punishments, only to be told that the culprit is none other than himself. David's lust for Bathsheba is to be avenged: Nathan prophesies that God will raise up "evil against thee out of thine own house" (12:10). The prophecy soon comes to pass: David's infant son dies (as did the Earnshaw son whose name was given to Heathcliff). Though this child will be replaced by Solomon, David's succession is undermined by incest, fraternal hatred, attempted usurpation: his son Amnon tries to violate his half-sister Tamar, and is killed at the instigation of her full brother Absalom, who will later try to overthrow his father. The discord bears distinct resemblances to that which will plague the

Earnshaws, where a patriarch's illicit lust may also have spawned fraternal jealousies and strife.

Yet Lockwood's first dream safely screens out such sordid materials. What adults brand and punish as sinful behaviour can be rendered harmless in a fantasy in which Lockwood becomes as a little child, albeit a rather rebellious little child. The staff of male power is not yet required, for it belongs to the realm of Experience, not Innocence. Play can still defuse what otherwise becomes punishable as an unpardonable transgression. But just as Catherine's amusing first diary entry set the stage for the far more serious and "lachrymose" events that followed, so do the seemingly innocuous materials contained in the first dream acquire ominous connotations when transported into the sexual nightmare that succeeds it. As Lockwood falls asleep again and dreams "more disagreeably than before," even Matthew 18 will re-enter his unconscious in a far more punitive fashion than before: "Woe unto the world because of offences! . . . Wherefore if thy hand or foot offend thee, cut them off, and cast them *from* thee: it is better for thee to enter into life halt or maimed, rather than having two hands or two feet to be cast into everlasting fire" (18:7–8). Severance or maiming is as much involved in Hindley's injunction against any further "play" between Catherine and Heathcliff as there is in Lockwood's desperate attempt to cut off the wrist of the "creature" who grips him as she tries to regain her former place in the old oak bed.

The mournful voice that frightens Lockwood claims having been "a waif for twenty years" (ch. 3). If so, this "child's face" belongs to one who is hardly a child anymore. Heathcliff's flight after overhearing the first half of Catherine's speech to Nelly took place in the summer of 1780, twenty years before, when Catherine was fifteen. Heathcliff had already slipped out when Catherine asked Nelly to lighten her "uncomfortable conscience" by reassuring her that her former playmate was still ignorant of such "things" as "being in love" (ch. 9). Catherine's reference here seems to be to a physical attraction such as that which draws her to Edgar. (One of the unfortunate consequences of the film versions of

Wuthering Heights in which the actor playing young Heathcliff is inevitably more handsome than Edgar has been a reversal of Brontë's quite contrary emphasis.)

Catherine lost Heathcliff, then, at an age comparable to that of the "waif" who wants to crawl back into the play-space the children had shared. When Nelly pointed out that Heathcliff would find "the separation" most difficult to bear, Catherine indignantly countered: "Who is to separate us, pray? They'll meet the fate of Milo!" (ch. 9). Ironically enough, she denies the separation that has already occurred. In education and in her sexual development she has outstripped the boy whom she still persists in regarding as an inseparable and inviolable part of her being. Even her bookish reference to the classical story of Milo − the aging athlete who was overpowered by a tree he tried to sever − ought to convince her how much she has moved beyond her backward companion.

Lockwood's imaginative alliance with the girl Catherine, sustained in the all-male scenario of his first dream, breaks down as soon as she materializes as a female. Not only are the former allies now cast as antagonists, but their gender-roles also become curiously reversed. The phallic staff that Lockwood wanted to wrest away from Joseph has become the "little ice-cold hand" that penetrates the broken window-pane and threatens to violate the dream-space of the young man I earlier called male, though unmasculine. In trying to repulse his invader, Lockwood assumes the posture Catherine assumed when she turned from defensiveness to outright offense. Finding the curtain of pinafores insufficient to withstand Joseph's assault, she revenged herself by attacking the books he had thrust at her. Lockwood's reaction, as he admits, is far more cruel. He tries to cut off the wrist on the broken glass, rubbing it "to and fro." Unable to loosen the "tenacious gripe" of the invader through this desperate act of mutilation, he resorts to language as his mode of defense: "How can I?," he expostulates, when the voice wails to be let in. "Let *me* go, if you want me to let you in" (ch. 3). His deception works. Whereas, before, Lockwood had shared the children's contempt for a perversion of the Word, he now relies on linguistic manipulation. It hardly seems coincidental that he should quickly gather the books he had deemed offensive in order to plug the gaping "hole" left by the child's withdrawing hand. Lockwood no longer resists Joseph's tracts. The texts he mocked for their negativity have become his new allies.

Lockwood's second dream allows Emily Brontë to anticipate what the unfolding narrative of Catherine's and Heathcliff's separation will then dramatize: the fall from oneness brought about by sexual maturation and by the acquisition of language. To become as little children again, Catherine and Heathcliff must vacate the reality in which Lockwood will continue to flounder. The spectre Lockwood perceived as a threat to his own dubious integrity will have to be fearlessly embraced. The integration Heathcliff wants to retrieve cannot be obtained in a world in which children turn into sexual and power-hungry adults.

Brothers and sisters

Despite the explanation I have advanced, there remains something curiously excessive about Lockwood's terrified repudiation of the dream-child who tries to creep into his bed. The dispossessed creature seems pitiful. She is not a ghoul or a vampire. Why should contact with someone Lockwood had regarded so sympathetically evoke such disgust? He might just as easily have offered shelter to the cold girl. In his *Confessions of an English Opium-Eater*, Thomas De Quincey remembered how, as an adolescent wanderer, he once welcomed a "forlorn" female child who "crept close to me for warmth, and for security against ghostly enemies." Snuggled together in an icy garret, under an "old sofa-cover, a small piece of rug, and some fragments of other articles, which added a little to our warmth," the girl and her older companion found temporary solace, though not the total symbiosis De Quincey prefers to seek in dreams. There, he expects to recover a lost sororal self, a female figure he can embrace as intensely and "as affectionately as if she had been my sister." What makes Brontë's dreamer resistant to what both his predecessor in the *Confessions* and the later Heathcliff find so irresistible?

Brontë teases us with the enigma she sets up so early in her novel. Like the confused Lockwood, the reader has been encouraged to press onward into the puzzling relations the Heights offers. And yet, just when our joint probe has taken us to the very center of this defensive structure of relations — to the space of Catherine's oak bed — we are denied a fuller access to its significance. Having invited us to watch most closely what has transpired in the recesses of Lockwood's dreams, Brontë now implicates us in the mechanisms of repression. Though Lockwood is forced to confide to Heathcliff that he has encountered Catherine's ghost, he disguises the violence of his response through a veneer of jocularity. And he conceals the encounter altogether from Nelly Dean, once back at the Grange. Nelly herself, it soon becomes evident, is even more adept in the art of concealment. She barely hints at elements that might reveal more about her own inner life: her early relations to both old Earnshaw and Hindley, for instance. Like the chastened Lockwood, our new guide prefers the public over the private. She quashes the important confessions Catherine tries to articulate, and gives but a partial hearing to Heathcliff's feverish communication of meanings which he, too, can at best express in a language that remains idiosyncratic and intimate. Something resembling the transgression that brought ruin to King David's children may lurk at the Heights. The irrational patriarch who imports an alien child may well be guilty of some dire offence, as I have suggested. If so, however, the name of the sin that no Christian need pardon will stay veiled.

Just as Lockwood fears the ghost as a sexual intruder, so will he resist Nelly's attempts to interest him in the alluring Cathy. *Wuthering Heights* may end with the conventional closure of a wedding. But, like the film versions which have erased Cathy and Hareton from the popular mind, the text itself prefers to stress the unconsummated desire it locates in the plight of the separated Catherine and Heathcliff. The sexual consummation of marriage is consistently depicted as dangerous by Brontë. Hindley's passion for the tubercular Frances, Catherine's physical attraction to Edgar, Isabella's infatuation with Heathcliff prove equally ruinous. Although, as I stressed in chapter 2, these unions ultimately strengthen the Earnshaw line, they benefit only the cousins who wed at the end. Why *do* Cathy and Hareton fare so much better than those who married outside their immediate families? The lovers with the eyes of Hindley and Catherine are, in effect, a brother and a sister, once removed. What would constitute an incestuous union for their parents is permissible for them; fraternal love and sexual love can become one and the same. As Cathy remarks at one point to her other cousin, Linton Heathcliff, whose virgin-widow she becomes until she molds Hareton into a better replacement: "people hate their wives, sometimes; but not their sisters and brothers, and if you were the latter you would live with us, and papa would be as fond of you as he is of me" (ch. 23).

Novels rely on tissues of relations through which an author transmits meanings which require further translation by the rearranging reader. The word "relation" itself, significantly, stems from the Latin name for an act of recovery in which old associations are brought back or transferred into a new domain. Let us rehearse for a moment the personal relations that shaped Emily Brontë's life before she created the fictive relations of *Wuthering Heights*. Emily was hardly three years old when her mother declined and died of cancer. The child's primary relation thus had to be supplanted by secondary ones. Although Emily never accepted her aunt Branwell with the docility shown by her younger sister Anne, she appears to have identified more strongly than any one of her surviving three siblings with her father.

The Reverend Patrick Brontë's features are discernible in the stern, irrational, yet loving portrait of Catherine's father that is softened when Edgar adopts the role of Cathy's "papa." Yet, as an Irishman, he also retained a sense of himself as an outsider, which his daughter shared and passed on to the alien Heathcliff. Himself the author of several volumes of poems (none as distinguished as Emily's), he seems to have early understood (though he can hardly be said to have later much encouraged) the creative precocity of his six extraordinary children. After the last of these had died, Mr Brontë remembered having extracted narratives from them by allowing them to hide their identity. His account, which Elizabeth Gaskell reproduced in her *Life of Charlotte Brontë*, goes back to a time when all six children, including the older Maria and Elizabeth, were still together. He had, he recalls, become the "arbitrator" of their arguments "as their mother was then dead." Paradoxically, it was upon intervening in the children's disputes that Mr Brontë professes to have discovered the first "signs of rising talent, which I had seldom or never before seen in any of their age." And to test that talent, he offered them the protection of a mask such as that which his daughters later employed when they concealed their identity as Acton, Ellis, and Currer Bell:

A circumstance now occurs to my mind which I may as well mention. When my children were very young, when, as far as I can remember, the oldest was about ten years of age, and the youngest about four, thinking that they knew more than I had yet discovered, in order to make them speak with less timidity, I deemed that if they were put under a sort of cover I might gain my end, and happening to have a mask in the house, I told them all to stand and speak boldly from under the cover of the mask.

(*The Life of Charlotte Brontë*, ch. 3).

Mr Brontë's reliance on this mask to make his children "speak" bears a distinct resemblance to another paternal gift that unloosened the tongues of the four children still left to him after the deaths of Maria and Elizabeth. The toy soldiers which his son Branwell shared with Charlotte, Emily, and Anne in 1826 stimulated the creative games that soon led to the stories, poems, histories, and dramas which for a decade and a half became, as Fannie E. Ratchford puts it, "the epic cycle of an imaginary world in which the four young Brontë's lived, moved, and had their being" (*The Brontë's Web of Childhood*, New York, 1941). If, in the first instance, a

father-mentor probed into the children's knowledge, his gift
to Branwell stimulated something that proved to be far more
precious: the fertile and uninhibited creative collaboration of
the four children who interacted with each other through fictive "relations." The play-space in which a mother gradually
conditions her child to confront the separations that accompany growth was thus appropriated by the children
themselves. Crucial to their emotional well-being, their imaginative games had a double effect. Play acted as a
pleasurable counterweight to their deprivation in a world of
reality; yet, at the same time, it also made that actuality seem
inferior to, and more problematic than, the fantasy-world
that had been so sustaining. Although all four children were
caught between these competing realities, the oldest and the
youngest, Charlotte and Anne, eventually accepted the compromises and accommodations the two middle children,
Branwell and Emily, found difficult to manage. That difference, as we shall eventually see, has a bearing on *Wuthering Heights*, as well as on Charlotte's and Anne's responses
to the book.

Let us, however, first look at the novel's incorporation of
the paternal perspective I have introduced through Mr.
Brontë. Unlike *Jane Eyre*, where the loss of her father and her
Uncle Reed makes Jane doubly deprived, *Wuthering Heights*
opens its "Earnshaw Chronicle" with the figure of a domi-
nant patriarch. And, what is more, this father imitates
Mr. Brontë when he too becomes the catalyst for the play
activities that bond two of the four children at his home. Mr.
Brontë brought Branwell the gift the boy shared with his three
sisters. Old Earnshaw, however, brings the three children at
his home, not the gifts he had promised, but a fourth child.
The situation in which a father distributes gifts to his offspring has many literary precedents. It occurs in fairy tales
such as "Beauty and the Beast" and "Aschenputtel" (the
Grimms' version of "Cinderella," which both Emily and
Charlotte seemed to have preferred to Perrault's); it sets the
stage in *King Lear* (that other fiction of relations gone awry,
on which *Wuthering Heights* so heavily draws). In Brontë's

novel, as in these antecedents, the promised distribution of gifts only creates discord.

Old Earnshaw fails to satisfy the expectation of each of the children in his home: Hindley's fiddle is crushed, Cathy's whip has been lost, Nelly's apples and pears have been forgotten. The replacement for these unsatisfied wishes seems inadequate. The "dirty, ragged, black-haired boy" the returning father exhibits beneath his "great coat" is himself hungry and unsated. Old Earnshaw thrusts this additional child, not at his disappointed brood, but at his protesting wife. Aggressively, he commands her to "take it as a gift of God, though it's dark almost as if it came from the devil" (ch. 4). Only Catherine, herself a little demonist, will welcome the "stupid little thing" she initially opposed as much as Hindley, Nelly, and her mother. Her allegiance is to the father. Just as old Earnshaw continues to take "strangely" to Heathcliff, preferring him over his legal children, so does Catherine soon regard this "H." as a more fraternal extension of herself than the "H." who is her actual brother.

This fable about the troubled relations among four children and a father (for Mrs Earnshaw soon dies) strangely resembles a situation treated genially by those who stress the benefits Mr Brontë's gift of toys brought to his imaginative youngsters. Although the causes of Hindley's and Nelly's resentment are clear, we are not told why Catherine and Heathcliff become attached to each other. When Nelly, whom Brontë has forced "out of the house," in a deliberate ellipsis, returns only "a few days afterwards," she finds that Catherine and the stranger have now become "very thick." What has endeared the boy to Catherine? He still speaks a language "nobody could understand," though he now has learned to "sleep with the children," as Old Earnshaw commanded. Does Catherine find his backwardness attractive? Though a year older than she (just as Branwell was a year older than Emily), he appears to accept domination by one who likes "to act the little mistress" (ch. 5). Has she, her father's former favourite, decided to regain some of Old Earnshaw's withdrawn love by identifying herself with his new love-object? Such explanations seem inadequate. For Brontë wants no causal clues to account for her book's arch-relation between male and female selves who claim that each *is* the other. Mystery must be maintained. Old Earnshaw's irrational attachment to the strange boy receives at least a partial justification: Nelly tells us what "little I could make out" of the account through which her "master tried to explain the matter" to his wife (ch. 4). But she seems totally uncurious about the genesis of Catherine's change of heart towards Heathcliff, in a relation that rivals (but exceeds) Nelly's own emotional identification with Hindley. She is content to inform us that Catherine "was much too fond of Heathcliff," and that "the greatest punishment we [Hindley and she?] could invent for her was to keep her separate from him" (ch. 5). The roots of the desire that will shape *Wuthering Heights* thus remain as carefully veiled as Heathcliff's own origins.

Who and *what* is Heathcliff? The question is asked by both Nelly and Isabella. Although Heathcliff is a character in his own right, he is as much the product of animated desire as that nameless sufferer from gender-bifurcations, the Frankenstein Monster. Shelley's creature, fashioned from the tissue of dead men (and women?), is an "it" until converted to male sadism. The boy whom old Earnshaw presents as an "it" is so denominated by Nelly no less than seventeen times until "he" is christened with a dead infant's name that "has served *him* ever since" (ch. 4). "Heathcliff" (the very name, like "Frankenstein," combining openness with hardness) thus exists, I would contend, essentially as part of a relation, first between child/parent and then, more intensely, of boy/girl selves. He is a metaphor made literal, enfleshed. Shaped by a world in which children must grow up and assume rigid identities, he feels betrayed. Only by returning into the metaphoric realm of essences into which Catherine precedes him can he confirm her credo: "I cannot express it," she had told Nelly; "but surely you and everybody have a notion that there is, or should be, an existence beyond you" (ch. 9). It seems hard not to hear Emily Brontë's own accents in this and similar utterances by Catherine and Heathcliff.

For *Wuthering Heights* registers, among other things, her disagreement with the two sisters who had come to accept their containment in a reality like Nelly Dean's.

What, then, is Heathcliff/Catherine? Their fusion, separation, and reintegration is cast through the form of kinship most frequently found in this novel of repetitions and redoublings, that of a brother and a sister. There are no less than six brother/sister pairs if we include cousins and foster-siblings:

literal	*metaphoric*	*literal/metaphoric*:
Hindley/Catherine	CATHERINE/HEATHCLIFF	Linton Heathcliff/Cathy
Edgar / Isabella	Nelly / Hindley	HARETON / CATHY

A seventh pair might be added to the other six in the shape of Nelly and Heathcliff. Whether or not these two outsiders are actually Old Earnshaw's illegitimate children is irrelevant. As Hindley's foster-sister and Catherine's foster-brother, the novel's main opponents automatically become each other's foster-siblings.

We have noted that the Hareton/Cathy marriage with which the "Earnshaw Chronicle" ends condenses Catherine's relations to her two "brothers," Heathcliff and Hindley; the union between Nelly's prime nursling and her foster-brother's son also produces a consummation, once removed, between Nelly and Hindley. Edgar and Isabella, that other alienated pair of siblings, can be said to "marry" each other through the brief union of their children, when Cathy becomes Linton Heathcliff's bride, in what can also be considered as still another surrogate espousal between Heathcliff and Catherine. The permutations of this central metaphor of fusing and diffusing brother/sister selves so overwhelm us by their variety that we give our relieved assent to the final contractions of Cathy/Hareton and Catherine/Heathcliff.

If, as I have been suggesting, Emily Brontë's fable of childhood lost and regained stems from her desire to reassert the violated imaginative oneness she once shared with her siblings, it seems unclear at first why she would not have chosen to portray her four children, as her sister Charlotte did in *Jane Eyre*, as three sisters and one brother. In her own tale about a disempowered Cinderella, Charlotte twice situates Jane into a domestic foursome. As a child, Jane is rejected by her Reed cousins, Eliza, Georgiana, and John, the offspring of her mother's brother; as an adult, however, she is welcomed by her Rivers cousins, Diana, Mary, and St. John, the children of her father's sister. Both the grotesque John Reed and the handsome St. John are unacceptable as sexual partners. For, unlike Cathy (who finds happiness through Hareton), Jane must wed someone who is not a blood relation. The taint of incest that in some societies still attaches to the marriage of cousins thus can be safely avoided. Charlotte, after all, wants to invest Jane with social, rather than primitive or asocial, powers. Emily, on the other hand, invests Heathcliff's abdication of all power with the same intense pleasure Jane experiences after she gains control over her maimed lover. Jane's erotic passion for Rochester, sanctioned only after his crippling, manifests itself in Emily's novel only when Heathcliff becomes free to make love to a sisterly ghost. In this sense, *Wuthering Heights* and *Jane Eyre* are affirmations of exactly contrary realities.

Biography, which so often has had the unfortunate effect of displacing the fictions written by the three Brontë sisters with fables of its own, can only go so far in elucidating the patterns of relation I have been tracing in this chapter. Yet, just as Charlotte Brontë deemed it necessary to introduce her sister's novel with a ''Biographical Notice,'' so must we remain alert to the shared (and disputed) ''web of childhood'' out of which *Wuthering Heights* is spun. The incestual patternings noted by critics such as Kavanagh (who somewhat incongruously interprets Lockwood's rejection of the ghost-child as an ''Oedipal father's refusal of sexual otherness'') or Karen Chase (in a thoughtful but unpublished lecture called ''After Incest'') are undeniably encoded in the book. And, as in several of the many Romantic lyrics and narratives that also rely heavily on this trope, the fictional relations represented involve, just as undeniably, a transformation of biographical relations. That process of transformation can easily be misinterpreted. We need, therefore, to proceed most guardedly in the final section of this chapter. For there, in what corresponds to the play-space Emily Brontë so zealously protected, we will try to understand the importance for her imagination of the irreparably broken brother she nursed while writing *Wuthering Heights*.

Sister and brother

Patrick Branwell Brontë, soon called "Branwell" after the second maternal name displaced the "patrician" and Irish name he shared with his father, had been Charlotte's, and not Emily's, prime creative partner in the children's imaginative games. It is therefore highly significant that he should have been totally excised from Charlotte's account at the start of her 1850 "Biographical Notice": "About five years ago, my two sisters and myself, after a somewhat prolonged period of separation, found ourselves reunited, and at home." Since a shattered Branwell also returned "home" in 1845, and since his decline and death in September 1848, less than three months before Emily's and eight months before Anne's, had such a powerful impact on his two young sisters, it seems all the more curious that the oldest should exclude him from her "Notice" of Acton and Ellis Bell. Instead, Charlotte insists on describing a sisterly collaboration from which any reference to the originator of their earlier collaborative games is pointedly omitted.

To this day, we remain unsure whether Branwell, who gave up on his own planned novel, entitled *And the Weary Are At Rest*, around the same time that his sisters were reviving their creative interactions, had any inkling about the appearance in print of the pseudonymous brothers Bell. Charlotte steadfastly maintained that the secret was rigorously kept from her brother until his death. Branwell's male friends, on the other hand, claimed that he had boasted himself to be the author of *Wuthering Heights*. As Winifred Gérin suggests in her *Emily Brontë* (Oxford, 1971), the truth appears to lie between these contrary assertions. It seems doubtful that

Charlotte could have prevented Branwell from knowing that the poems and novels of his sisters had been published, an action designed, as she contended, to spare him "remorse for time misspent" (and also, one would assume, envy of the success denied to him). But even if her assertion is true, it seems clear from the evidence Gérin rehearses that Emily discussed her own writing with Branwell. Whether or not he ultimately knew that her novel appeared in print (or even cared to know) seems less important than his awareness of its existence in manuscript.

Though all critics of *Wuthering Heights* have dismissed Branwell's self-aggrandizing remarks about having authored the novel, some of them, including Q. D. Leavis, who speaks of "the influence of Branwell" on the text ("A Fresh Approach to *Wuthering Heights*," reprinted in the Norton Edition), are disposed to accept him as a shadowy collaborator. Percy Shelley, falsely credited with his wife's *Frankenstein*, was eventually shown to have written only the book's preface and, possibly, its last paragraph. This precedent has perhaps led to the conjecture that Branwell might have at least written the opening chapters of *Wuthering Heights*, a theory advanced by those who see affinities between Lockwood and Emily's insecure brother. The suggestion is preposterous, but it demonstrates how fully and convincingly Emily could impersonate such a male figure. If Lockwood's confusions and culminating nightmare, Hindley's erotic dependence on Frances and subsequent bouts of delirium, and Heathcliff's obsession with a sororal ghost are suggestive of Branwell's behaviour, it must be remembered that Emily observed his mental and physical breakdown with far greater empathy than either of her sisters could muster. Charlotte's first male impersonation in *The Professor* had been an abject failure, leading to the female "I" who speaks so forcefully through Jane Eyre. Emily's sympathy with a brother, however, led her to penetrate male psychology with an understanding that only George Eliot, among her female successors, was to carry further.

Branwell had no actual hand in shaping *Wuthering*

Heights. But Emily nonetheless saw in his decline an actualization of the same fall she would so brilliantly interpret and dramatize in her novel. In this sense, at least, he, more than her two sisters, had become her partner. The brother whose self-embodiment as the proud "Percy Northangerland" Charlotte had gleefully shared as a child needed to be discarded by the writer who would find her voice through the angry Jane Eyre. Yet his pathos, his very failure, had now made him an outlet for Emily's sympathetic imagination. She was not as offended by Branwell's derelictions as were the other members of her family. For she saw him less as a villain than as a victim of his forced entry into a world of sexuality and power in which he could no more succeed than Linton Heathcliff. Unlike his model De Quincey, Branwell could not master that socio-sexual reality because of his inability to retrieve a childhood sister-self.

That lost, complementary self was none of Branwell's three living sisters, but rather a child-ghost, a "waif" no living woman could replace. As mentioned in chapter 1, Branwell never overcame the deprivation he suffered upon the death of the oldest Brontë child, who bore his mother's first name (just as he would thereafter use his mother's maiden name instead of the paternal "Patrick"). Maria's death reactivated for the boy the pangs of his earlier separation, a loss she had helped ease by adopting her dead mother's role. But Branwell's need to experience fusion in a maternal play-space was once more relocated in the creative games he instigated. His three new partners, notably the older Charlotte, restored the pleasurable sense of separateness-in-oneness, until this fellowship, too, was broken up by the children's dispersion. Like Emily, Branwell resisted the erosion of this shared fantasy-world of childhood. But what Emily's imagination could soon hew into complex structures of resistance and accommodation, became for him little more than an occasion for maudlin exercises in nostalgia.

While Emily, who remained her father's main companion, soon wrote poems that stressed the fortitude and stoicism the elder Brontë had himself tried to celebrate in his own

published verses, Branwell continued his obsessive mourning
for Maria in poems as mawkish as the one Gérin reproduces
at great length in her 1961 *Branwell Brontë*. There, a "funeral
bell" rekindles the "childish fear" provoked by a sister's
death in a speaker who is neither a young man, nor a little
boy, but a little girl. In a gender-inversion that lacks the ironic
control of Emily's impersonation of the adolescent
Lockwood, Branwell assumes the guise of a tremulous
"Harriet" whose "mother mild" rather unwisely forces
her/him to stare "at *your* sister and my child / One moment,
ere her form be hid / For ever 'neath its coffin lid!" The conflation of mother and sister, the fixation on the perishable
"form" whose features might be erased (like Catherine Earnshaw's) once lowered into the grave, the transpositions of
gender and age which convert a twenty-year-old male into
little "Harriet," speak for themselves. And they help explain
Branwell's subsequent inability to function as an adult male
in the nineteenth-century order in which his father, with
greater disadvantages, had found a niche for himself.
Branwell's quest for a sister/mother led to his disastrous
attachment to the married mother of the children he and Anne
were tutoring. When Mrs. Robinson, suddenly widowed,
preferred a wealthy and maturer mate to her childish lover,
Branwell's despair exceeded Heathcliff's on discovering
Catherine's choice of Edgar Linton.

Yet Branwell possessed none of the resilience of the fictional figure whom Emily invested with her own fierce
energies. Instead, his latest separation compounded the
earlier losses he had suffered; his sense of betrayal made him
infantile again, a wounded child. Anne and Charlotte were as
shocked by their brother's immaturity as by his other lapses
in decorum. Emily, however, recognizing the sources of his
plight, transmuted Branwell's story into the myth of
Catherine/Heathcliff and their dispersed selves. Whereas
Branwell was now barred from participating in the creative
lives of his other two sisters, it was only proper for Emily,
usually so closed and private, to allow him a renewed access
to her own imagination. He was not the "author" of

Wuthering Heights, nor could ever have been. But inasmuch as her book was the product of a mind who understood the import of the resemblances between her and him, Emily's story of childhood Eden lost was, as she so generously acknowledged, also very much his own.

In the Reverend Patrick Brontë's account of his questioning of the six children he had sheltered with the mask of anonymity, the replies given by Emily and Branwell clearly stand out from the others:

I began with the youngest (Anne, afterwards Acton Bell), and asked what a child like her most wanted; she answered, "Age and experience." I asked the next (Emily, afterwards Ellis Bell), what I had best do with her brother Branwell, who was sometimes a naughty boy; she answered, "Reason with him, and when he won't listen to reason, whip him." I asked Branwell what was the best way of knowing the difference between the intellects of men and women; he answered, "By considering the difference between them as to their bodies." I then asked Charlotte what was the best book in the world; she answered, "The Bible." And what was the next best; she answered, "The Book of Nature." I then asked the next [Elizabeth] what was the best mode of education for a woman; she answered, "That which would make her rule her house well." Lastly, I asked the oldest [Maria] what was the best mode of spending time; she answered, "By laying it out in preparation for a happy eternity." I may not have given precisely their words, but I have nearly done so, as they made a deep and lasting impression on my memory. The substance, however, was exactly what I have stated.

(Gaskell, *The Life of Charlotte Brontë*, ch. 3)

Despite its final protestation, the account may be shaped by a father's hindsight of the fates of each of his dead children. Nonetheless, it remains a remarkable document. Only Emily and Branwell are asked to comment about other human relations; the others are all invited to come up with abstractions about experience, authority, discipline, and futurity. Emily's and Branwell's answers possess the specificity and physical concreteness the others lack. If "reason" cannot move a naughty boy, Emily hints, a whip may have the desired effect on his body. Branwell provides a rejoinder to Emily as much as a reply to his father's question. If reason cannot settle how a girl's mind differs from a boy's, a peek at their bodies might resolve the question. The forebodings seem ironic. Branwell's creative pretensions came to naught when, as a grownup male, he could not survive in a world of gender differences. Emily's male whip, on the other hand, figures prominently in the novel in which her intellect proved its superiority. The whip Catherine had expected to receive from her father was replaced by the boy named Heathcliff after "a son who had died in childhood" (ch. 4).

In chapter 12 of *Wuthering Heights* Catherine describes the regressive fit she underwent when, "most strangely, the last seven years of my life grew a blank." She has lost "command of tongue, or brain," as she shrunk back into childhood, lying at the Grange "with my head against that table leg," yet thinking herself once more "enclosed in the oak-panelled bed at home." For a moment, time has been collapsed:

> I was a child; my father was just buried, and my misery arose from the separation that Hindley had ordered between me and Heathcliff. I was laid alone, for the first time, and, rousing from a dismal doze after a night of weeping, I lifted my hand to push the panels aside: it struck the table-top! I swept it along the carpet, and then memory burst in − my late anguish was swallowed in a paroxysm of despair.
> (ch. 12)

Fantasy and memory are opposed in this passage. The latter reminds the child who had been forced to sleep alone that she has become "converted" into "Mrs. Linton." Having looked backward, aware that she can never be "a girl again, half savage and hardy," Catherine now looks forward. She beholds Nelly as "an aged woman" with "grey hair, and bent shoulders," an emblem of Experience. She predicts Nelly's further deformation into a witch-like, "withered hag": "That's what you'll come to fifty years hence" (ch. 12).

The death-wish that propels first Catherine and then Heathcliff to escape a "withering" world of Experience acts as an antidote to Nelly's compromises. Nonetheless, *Wuthering Heights* also endorses Nelly's repeated affirmations of life: when the delirious Hindley tries to ram a knife down her throat, his foster-sister laughingly tells him that she dislikes the fishy taste of the blade (ch. 9). But such resistances ebbed in real life, as Emily had to confront her brother's ravings and death-threats, and carry him bodily to his room. Gérin's moving account of what Branwell's deterioration and death meant to Emily needs to be fully read if we are to grasp why his sister willed her death so shortly after his own (*Emily Brontë*, pp. 242–7).

Emily Brontë refused to be shattered by the reality that had thwarted Branwell. She would not, as he had done, seek the embodiment of desire in a material world. Nor would she compromise that desire, as she felt that Charlotte and Anne had done. There was an alternative path, and she had laid it out for Heathcliff. She would retain her integrity by entering the realm of the imagination. Thus, paradoxically, at the very pinnacle of her artistic powers, she chose to extinguish those powers by ending her Nelly-like hold on life. Her novel's lack of appreciative readers only facilitated the final process of disengagement. All of Emily Brontë's tenacity was now deployed in the service of something very much resembling Heathcliff's fierce conviction that only death could reunite him with the object of his desire, and make him whole again.

Chapter 4

The after-life of *Wuthering Heights*

Unquiet ghosts

Wuthering Heights closes on an ambiguous note. The book's open ending suggests the co-existence of alternative explanations: Lockwood's (and Nelly's) quietism remains at odds with a belief in the animation of the ghosts of Catherine and Heathcliff seen by a Blakean child-shepherd. The lingering after-image of those roaming spectres affects our responses to the entire book. We want to settle the last of the enigmas with which we have been confronted. We thus either give our assent to the continued stir of Catherine/Heathcliff, or, persuaded by the lyricism of the novel's last sentence, we lay them to rest by refusing to imagine "unquiet slumbers for the sleepers in that quiet earth" (ch. 34). Our predilections may differ. But in either case, our eagerness to complete what Emily Brontë leaves unsettled suggests how profoundly she challenges her readers through her Shakesperean ability to keep opposites in suspension.

This challenge, I think, accounts for the survival and continued appeal of *Wuthering Heights*, generation after generation. Despite neglect by its first readers, the book soon found a place in the imaginations of writers who wrestled with the same contraries Emily Brontë had dramatized. Had she lived into the 1850s and 1860s, the novelist would have been surprised to witness her impact on such writers as Matthew Arnold and George Eliot. The many reprints of her novel in our century and its translation into other languages as well as other media would, of course, have seemed a chimerical impossibility.

Still, as the conflict between civilization and its discontents grew more marked, *Wuthering Heights* made further inroads.

Whereas the Victorians had still placed their faith in a social order which they viewed with increasing skepticism as the decades rolled by, the first World War exposed the anarchic underside of civilization. The negativism and violence that had alienated the 1847 reviewers of *Wuthering Heights* could still be held against a late-Victorian novel such as Thomas Hardy's *Jude the Obscure* (1895). Yet to twentieth-century readers, Brontë soon seemed to have been endowed with an uncanny prescience. Though her novel may still offend those who think that fiction "should be satisfied with imitating the surface of life," as L. P. Hartley puts it, "we live in an age of unreason and cannot, after what has recently happened in the world, and may happen again on a greater scale, refrain from inquiring what it is in human nature that makes such convulsions possible." In his shrewd remarks to the Brontë Society in 1965 ("Emily Brontë in Gondal and Gaaldine," *Brontë Society Transactions*, 14:5), Hartley hails *Wuthering Heights* for its "naked and uncompromising" presentation of "a perpetual need" for union in a destructive world:

Had humanity progressed, as the nineteenth century believed it would, with an ever-developing civility of life, then *Wuthering Heights* might have become a literary curiosity . . . But it has not. Experiences that have been real to us would have seemed utterly unreal to the most eminent Victorians; but not to Emily Brontë.

Hartley, himself a novelist, captures here Brontë's special appeal to the twentieth-century imagination. As he points out, the brutality which its Victorian reviewers had adduced against it can hardly unsettle the modern reader: "We, with the memory of the atom bomb and the concentration camp fresh in our minds, cannot pretend to be shocked by the pinchings, hair-pulling, puppy-hanging, slappings, by the elementary brutality of *Wuthering Heights*, itself an embryo concentration camp, and must respectfully agree with the author, who said that people who called it brutal must be affected." Even the toughness of Nelly Dean has acquired a special poignancy in times in which survival carries more urgent meanings than it did for the Victorians.

The shifting reception of *Wuthering Heights*, its interest to a readership affected by new ideas about sexuality and the unconscious, its acceptance as a carefully honed construct by intellectuals and as a popular romance (imitated in countless pulp novels) by the public at large, its canonization as a literary landmark by teachers, its special interest to film-makers, deserve to be thoroughly examined in what would become a rich and revealing chapter of Western cultural history. What follows in these last pages is much more modest. I want to suggest but a few ways in which Brontë's novel filtered into the productions of later writers and artists. These later works inevitably contribute to our understanding of *Wuthering Heights* itself. Whether fashioned by Brontë's near-contemporaries or by more distant successors, they respond to the tensions that shape her book. Yet a clear distinction emerges: whereas the Victorians try to tame the energies they recognize, the modernists prefer to stress the novel's anarchic or libidinal powers. By asserting one extreme at the expense of its contrary, such revisions necessarily violate what Brontë keeps in suspension. But if her dialectic remains more compendious, its deformations are significant. For they remind us of the inexhaustibility of the myth she had fashioned. Future readers are bound to reinterpret *Wuthering Heights* again and again, disquieted by what cannot be laid to rest. The book will continue to provoke through its uncompromising refusal to yield the very synthesis it encourages us to desire.

Victorian domestications

The immediate impact of *Wuthering Heights* can be detected in the work of three major writers whose literary identities were still in a transitional state in the 1850s: Charlotte Brontë, Matthew Arnold, and George Eliot. As "editor" of the 1850 version of the novel, Charlotte had a direct control of her sister's utterance; yet her continued dialogue with *Wuthering Heights* is evident in *Villette* (1853), where she reviewed the emotional impact of her and Emily's 1842 sojourn in Brussels. As a late-born Romantic poet, Matthew Arnold saw

Emily Brontë as an alter ego he needed to leave behind for his successful self-translation from a mournful elegist into a prose polemicist and witty apostle of "Culture." Finally, Marian Evans, who transformed herself from anonymous essayist into the pseudonymous author of novels hailed in their own time as much as today, acknowledged her debt to both Charlotte and Emily as sister-novelists when she adopted the name of "Eliot": a version of the prophetic "Elihu," previously assumed by Lamb's "Elia," Emily Jane Brontë's "*Ellis* Bell," and Jane Eyre's own self-masking as "Jane Elliot."

Before we look at some of the ways in which *Wuthering Heights* affected these writers, we must briefly consider an imaginative response which preceded theirs, namely, Anne Brontë's *The Tenant of Wildfell Hall*, published in June 1848, when both Branwell and Emily were still alive. In her own efforts to gain fictional control over the emotional drama of Branwell's unfulfilled longing for a female Other, Anne tried to feminize her sister's novel. Both books start with a young male narrator curious about the identity of the main occupant of a nearby building. In each case that building is given a double name, which bears the same initials, "W. H.," and which is deemed significant enough to be placed in each novel's title. But the Lockwoodian narrator of *Wildfell Hall* is not mesmerically drawn to a male more potent than he, but rather is attracted to an equally enigmatic female tenant, Helen Huntingdon, whom he will eventually be grown enough to marry. For her part, the married Helen is a Catherine who does not give in to a morbid death-wish. Although she too has been imprudent in her choice of husband, she resolutely parries the brute who, far from resembling the mild Edgar, is a sadistic Heathcliffian who teaches their infant son to drink and to curse his mother (in an intensification of Hareton's schooling by his "devil daddy"). Brother–sister relations, too, proliferate in *Wildfell Hall*. But the fusion between such selves is avoided: Gilbert, the narrator, must dearly pay for distrusting Helen when he mistakes her brother for a rival lover.

The Tenant of Wildfell Hall is certainly more than "Anne's poor shade of *Wuthering Heights*," as Lawrence and E. M. Hansen unfairly call the book in their *The Four Brontës* (London, p. 233). Still, the novel's vitality stems from the male anarchism it wants to soften. The debauched Arthur Huntingdon and his more sinister doubles, all of whom bear names which, like Hindley's, Heathcliff's, and Hareton's, begin with "H.," are clearly derived from their fictional counterparts in *Wuthering Heights*, though similarly grounded in Branwell's observed behaviour. Anne's feminization of what she regarded as Emily's excessive identification with male sadism hinges on her idealization of Helen Huntingdon. The love/hatred attracting Catherine and Heathcliff was that of co-equal selves, charged with the same intensity. But the union between the adolescent Gilbert and the mature Helen only helps to magnify her superiority. Since his Lockwoodian subservience to a mother's strong opinions and Helen's own exemplary mothering of her little boy have been stressed from the start, it becomes obvious that, at the novel's close, Gilbert is being granted the maternal surrogate whom Branwell never found – and Heathcliff never sought – within an ideal family circle. The ending of *Wildfell Hall* thus has a Lockwood marry, not a provocative Cathy, but a Nelly Dean, now elevated into a nurturing angel of domesticity.

For Charlotte Brontë, who links the "unfavourable reception" of *Wildfell Hall* to that of *Wuthering Heights* in her "Biographical Notice of Acton and Ellis Bell" of 1850, "Anne's choice of subject was an entire mistake," at odds with her "nature" as a writer and as "a very sincere and practical Christian." Charlotte hints that Anne should never have ventured into Emily's domain. In a veiled reference to Branwell, Charlotte goes on to explain the causes for Anne's mistaken effort:

The motives which dictated this choice were pure, but, I think, slightly morbid. She had, in the course of her life, been called on to contemplate, near at hand and for a long time, the terrible effect of talents misused and faculties abused; hers was naturally a sensitive, reserved, and dejected nature; what she saw sank very deeply into her mind; it did her harm. She brooded over it till she believed it to be a duty to reproduce every detail (of course with fictitious characters, incidents, and situations) as a warning to others.

Charlotte's reasons for discussing *Wildfell Hall* rather than *Agnes Grey*, the novel she was reissuing with *Wuthering Heights*, should now be clear. She has her own "warning" to make: Anne's imagination should not have touched materials already processed by one more "morbid," and also far more powerful, than she. It is Emily's imagination, rather than Anne's "motives" or Branwell's "abused" faculties, that haunts the last surviving Brontë child.

The challenge that *Wuthering Heights* posed for Charlotte Brontë went far beyond that which had led the well-meaning Anne to construct her counterfiction about a this-worldly female saint. Emily's was a rival imagination that Charlotte both admired and needed to subdue. Their ideologies, as I have suggested before, were inimical. Although both *Wildfell Hall* and *Wuthering Heights* may have struck Charlotte as accusatory reminders of her own unbending rejection of the brother who had been her prime creative partner, Emily's challenge lay elsewhere. Anne's infection by demonism thus merely is used to anticipate the severer warning issued in the "Editor's Preface to the New Edition of *Wuthering Heights*": "Whether it is right or advisable to create beings like Heathcliff, I do not know: I scarcely think it is. But this I know; the writer who possesses the creative gift owns something of which he is not always a master − something that strangely wills and works for itself." The sister whom Charlotte here masculinizes into a "he" has allowed herself to become possessed by a male demon whose self-destructiveness is dangerous because it is seductive. Charlotte had resisted that seductiveness. The unfulfilled desire so powerfully eroticized and yet mastered in *Jane Eyre* was something she was not willing to turn against her own psyche in an act of self-annihilation. The unselfconsciousness of the writer who allowed herself to be mastered by her "creative gift" deeply disturbed the selfconscious writer who had capitalized on the inviolable "I" of Jane Eyre.

Charlotte Brontë, therefore, set out to repossess the dead but defiant sister-self who had allowed herself to be possessed by Heathcliff. That repossession took a variety of shapes, some of which, like the adoption of a Lockwoodian persona in the "Editor's Preface" or the conversion of Nelly Dean and Edgar Linton into homiletic "specimens" of virtue, we have already had occasion to examine. Charlotte tampered with *Wuthering Heights* in other ways, as well, and also with Emily's poems. As Masao Miyoshi, who has carefully compared the 1850 text to the first edition of the novel, notes, Charlotte's editing "amounts virtually to a writing down, a taming of the novel." By altering Emily's diction, she often diluted the intensity of earlier phrasings: she changed "thick" to the more genteel "intimate," replaced "Give over, Isabella" with "Hush, Isabella," and strained to make Joseph's vernacular more accessible, thereby creating as Miyoshi well puts it, "a grotesque non-speech" mixing the polite and the uncouth. Her changes in punctuation imposed regularity on rhythms that were idiosyncratic, yet effective.

More disturbing than her editorial control over the novel or her refashioning of the seventeen poems (out of 193) by Emily that she chose to present to a Victorian audience, however, was the ruthless censorship that Charlotte exercised over the memory of a sister. Emily's reclusive nature had already made her less known than the siblings who had moved in wider social circles. Was it "overanxiety to protect Emily's privacy," as Barbara and Gareth Lloyd Evans maintain, that led Charlotte to destroy, "with typical efficiency," every scrap she could find of Emily's correspondence and diaries? (*The Scribner Companion to the Brontës*: New York, 1982, p. 113). The Evanses admit that we cannot know for certain "that this act happened, only that it is feasible." Its feasibility seems to be supported by the complete absence of Emily's prose juvenilia. Whereas reams of Branwell's and Charlotte's stories have survived, Emily's (and Anne's) seem to have disappeared. The existence of Emily's French *devoirs*, written in Brussels, and the testimonials about her superiority of intellect delivered, ironically enough, by the same Belgian master with whom Charlotte had so hopelessly fallen in love, are therefore all the more valuable. They help to counter the portrait of an unworldly and insulated, "homebred country girl," a rustic "nun," which Charlotte presents in her "Editor's Preface," and which was then picked up and disseminated by Mrs Gaskell in her *Life of Charlotte Brontë*.

Since it had been at the Brussels *pensionnat* where the differences in temperament between the two sisters first manifested themselves so openly, it is hardly surprising that Charlotte's reworking of these experiences in her third novel, *Villette*, should once more have led her to confront *Wuthering Heights*. *Villette* has rightly been considered as a reworking of *Jane Eyre* (as well as of the unsuccessful first novel, *The Professor*, which Charlotte wrote while Emily was working on *Wuthering Heights*). What critics have not sufficiently considered, however, are the strong points of contact between Charlotte's third and last major work of fiction and Emily's only novel. Unlike the ever-honest Jane Eyre, the "I" who narrates *Villette* is as unreliable as Nelly Dean. Lucy Snowe suppresses information. Tightly locked into her own mind, she is a version of the tough, unworldly creature Charlotte had portrayed in the 1850 "Editor's Preface." Charlotte had already endowed Shirley Keeldar, the heroine of *Shirley* (1849), with some of Emily's traits. Lucy Snowe, however, is an attempted conflation, a reconciliation, of Emily and Charlotte. Now fused into a single fictional self, as Catherine and Heathcliff had blended, this condensation re-experiences events to which they had reacted quite differently when experienced in real life.

The disorientation which Lockwood induces in the reader who has wandered into *Wuthering Heights* becomes even more pronounced in the opening pages of *Villette*. Important emotional responses are repressed; transitions are punched out. Lockwood finds his bearings under Nelly's guidance, but the reader of *Villette* remains baffled by Lucy's concealments. Even Lockwood's rejection of a dead little girl is given a new, disturbing twist at the start of *Villette*, when we witness a living little girl's touching pleas for affection from a Lockwoodian adolescent, without being allowed an emotional access to this relation. The cool detachment with which Lucy handles such unbearably painful scenes of separation and desire suggest how skillfully Charlotte could adapt her sister's distancing techniques in a fiction in which she tapped the emotional core of *Wuthering Heights*. Yet she also remained true to her own ideology. The "withering" storms that blow in *Villette* as much as in Emily's novel enable a reconstituted, strengthened female self to survive without desiring a male complement.

If *Villette* is an elegy that confers strength on a surviving self, so is Matthew Arnold's "Haworth Churchyard: Written April, 1855," a poem in which a stranger appropriates the ghosts of the "sisterly band" to come to terms with his own artistic identity. The poem is shaped by Arnold's understanding of *Wuthering Heights*, an understanding vaguely apparent in his earlier "The Scholar-Gipsy" in which a Lockwoodian young man both covets yet keeps at a distance the ghost of a simpler, purer past, freely moving in an ever-open landscape. In "Haworth Churchyard," however, such affinities are far more overt. The speaker now *is* a Lockwood detained by graves. But, unlike Lockwood, he wants to record his kinship with one more uncompromising than he, the true Romantic he represents as a female Byron and whose language he enlists for the poem's closure.

Arnold introduces the four Brontës in the order of their sojourn among the living: he addresses the recently dead Charlotte; passes by the "sweet and graceful," but less "puissant," Anne; hits the poem's highest pitch with his tribute to Emily; and ends with Branwell, a failure, "the child / Of many hopes, of many tears," his fellow-male, "a boy." The strategy serves him well. For the final pairing allows Arnold to enlist Emily/Branwell as a mirror to view himself, his own aspirations and fears. Branwell is cast as a Strayed Reveller, a poet *manqué*, a version of the "foolish boy" on whom the powerful Circe had frowned in Arnold's first major poem.

Emily, on the other hand, has a Circe's metamorphic powers: every bit as daring as Byron, "the world-famed son of fire," she pays a bitter price for the exercise of her masculine imagination, sinking to the grave, "Baffled, unknown, self-consumed."

Emily's "too bold song" stirs the fellow singer standing by these graves, but also frightens him by its intensity. Hovering between two poetic identities, a female Byron and a boyish dreamer, one dead, the other never destined to be born, Arnold opts for neither. He can wed them – and be wedded to them – only through the tribute shaped by his more cautious, divided imagination. Yet even his tribute is found wanting. In an "Epilogue," a frowning "Muse" appears to silence this singer and ask him to end his song. Chided by this stern female for attempting to rival the compositions of sister imaginations superior to his own, Arnold resorts to Emily Brontë's closure for *Wuthering Heights* to help him close his own poem. By rearranging her words and losing himself in them, he can at least follow her by also losing himself in the impersonality of a Yorkshire landscape:

> April showers
> Rush o'er the Yorkshire moors.
> Stormy, through driving mist,
> Loom the blurr'd hills; the rain
> Lashes the newly-made grave.
>
> Unquiet souls!
> – In the dark fermentation of earth,
> In the never idle workshop of nature,
> In the eternal movement,
> Ye shall find yourselves again!

Remembering Charlotte's words about the "wild workshop" in which *Wuthering Heights* was hewn, Arnold relies on the elementary nature into which the ghosts of Catherine and Heathcliff had blended, to assure us that, contrary to Lockwood's protestations, the blending Brontë imaginations will never be quieted, but remain astir. His own stirred imagination thus can at least coalesce with theirs.

Around the same time that this urbane elegist was entombing his creative aspirations in Haworth churchyard, George Eliot entered the rustic "workshop" the Brontës had vacated through her own fictional revisitations of lost childhood landscapes. Just as the three Brontë sisters had set out by writing shorter works (of which *Wuthering Heights* proved to be the longest and most ambitious), so did the new novelist, encouraged by George Henry Lewes, Charlotte's erstwhile literary adviser, start her career with the three shorter pieces that eventually made up her *Scenes of Clerical Life* (1858). In the second of these, "Mr. Gilfil's Love-Story," the new writer, still influenced by Lewes's canons of realism, tries to tame Emily's romance while feeding on its energies. The romantic story of another Catherine – Caterina or Tina Sarti, an exotic child adopted by a country gentleman – is given a novel twist. Torn between two lovers – one aristocratic and handsome and a legal heir, the other lowbred and homely, himself adopted and dependent on patronage – Tina makes the right choice, yet nonetheless dies in childbirth, like Catherine Earnshaw, taking her child to the grave. Even more than Emily Brontë, George Eliot stresses the agonies of a male survivor. Like Heathcliff, the grieving Gilfil converts the dead woman's bedroom into a sanctuary. But Gilfil's ritual is the opposite of Heathcliff's. He wants the "Gothic casement of the oriel window" permanently shut. There are no haunted moors, no beckoning female ghosts. Instead, we are asked to confine our pity to a male ruin, a "poor lopped oak," deformed by the loss of the female who had been his childhood playfellow.

This calculated reversal of *Wuthering Heights* stems from affinities that George Eliot was not ready to treat more fully until she, too, was prepared to tell the story of separated brother/sister selves who could only be reunited through death. She carefully reread *Wuthering Heights* in 1858. The impact of her reading becomes evident in *The Mill on the Floss*, where Dorlcote Mill becomes, as much as the structure called Wuthering Heights, the site for a tragedy involving the loss of a childhood Eden. As in Brontë's story, the sundered brother and sister who cannot take their place in an adult civilization also have a father who, like Old Earnshaw, determines the irreversible course of events. George Eliot, however, fills in many of the causal explanations that Emily Brontë prefers to elide. The correlatives provided by history, genetics, education, human miscalculation, and human self-interest are enlisted by an author who knows that such explanatory systems are inadequate to account for the process she wants to interpret. Falling back on the "eternal movement" of uncontrollable natural forces which Arnold had invoked at the end of his poem, George Eliot summons the waters of the flooding river. The emotional over-spill on which she ends not only reunites her alienated brother and sister selves, but also helps her to drown the resistances posed by her extraordinary analytical mind to the myths of romance and transcendence. Still, the swirling waters allow Tom and Maggie to recover, only in the finite instant of their death, the fusion which Brontë's unquiet ghosts find within an eternity. The Miltonic erudition of the wisest of Victorian novelists does not permit her to reclaim the "paradise better far" a Brontë sister had boldly asserted. Intelligence repairs some ravages, but not all.

To Harriet Beecher Stowe, with whom George Eliot corresponded later in her career, the author of the *Mill on the Floss* and *Middlemarch* seemed nothing less than a reincarnation of Emily Brontë's ghost, eager to dictate further fictions to a passive amanuensis. The extravagant claim amused George Eliot. She was hardly an automaton "possessed" by Emily, as Charlotte had considered Emily to be possessed by Heathcliff. Yet it is true that their common interest in masculine psychology, patriarchs, and brother-selves made George Eliot's imagination closer to Emily's than those of Anne and even Charlotte had been. Such affinities notwithstanding, *Wuthering Heights* stands alone. Its attractions for these and other Victorian writers not considered here (Lewis Carroll, for example, or Thomas Hardy) lay precisely in its uniqueness. Like the productions of the Romantic writers of an earlier generation, the fiction of this sister-novelist posed a challenge. If *Wuthering Heights* could not be imitated, it needed at least to be confronted.

A fable for modernists

Wuthering Heights acquired a new status as a proto-modernist text when an assent to the temporal and material reality to which the mid-Victorians had still tried to cling became more and more problematic. Thus, it seems hardly coincidental that Emily Brontë's novel should recently have been paired with Lautréamont's *Les Chants de Maldoror*, in an important discussion of narrative metamorphoses by Leo Bersani. *Maldoror*, in which the narrator turns into a shark as well as into a pig, is shaped by "an imagination unconstrained by any responsibility to the real"; though no one changes into a shark in Nelly's controlled narrative, there is in *Wuthering Heights*, too, as Bersani shows, the same kind of "ontological slipperiness" that occurs when identities, pried loose from the real, can slide into one another (*A Future for Astyanax: Character and Desire in Literature*, Boston and Toronto, 1976, pp. 194, 196).

If the previous section was itself bound to a temporal reality by examining how *Wuthering Heights* affected writings that appeared in the twelve years following its first publication, this final section will be less constrained by historical sequence. To find the descendants of Catherine and Heathcliff in the modern novel is hardly difficult. In D. H. Lawrence's *Women in Love* (1920), for instance, Catherine's description of Heathcliff to Isabella as "a fierce, pitiless, wolfish man" is applied to Gerald Critch (ch. 10). The echo reminds us that Lawrence's antecedents are to be found, not just in *Wuthering Heights* itself, but in the intermediate fictions of George Eliot and Thomas Hardy on which he drew in his fable of sisters in search of male complements. At the end of *Women in Love* Lawrence follows Victorian precedent by entrusting his lovers to a "never idle workshop" of a nature that can unite as well as divide them. Like Cathy and Hareton, Ursula and Birkin are allowed to find fruition in a this-worldly order. But the reality that envelops them can also entomb others. The frozen body of Gerald Critch comes to symbolize, as did the stiffened corpses of Brontë's Heathcliff and Hardy's Jude, a desire that cannot be consummated in a material world. In his final metamorphosis into a stone, Gerald has become the petrified "human shape" which Charlotte Brontë equated with Heathcliff at the end of her 1850 Preface to *Wuthering Heights*. The human "crag" of Heathcliff's remains has been vacated by a spirit that has rejoined Catherine. In Gerald's case, however, that crag acts as a testimonial to the impossibility of attaining such a final metamorphosis. For Gudrun, his female double, remains obdurately alive. A sculptress, and hence like that sister "statuary" whose male "chisel" Charlotte feared, she has not been able to fulfill her desire. And nor has Birkin, who looks at the corpse of a brother-self, with something of that regretful longing with which Victorian elegists looked at Branwell.

Such narrative transformations can tell us much about the endurance of *Wuthering Heights* in the twentieth-century imagination. But the book's appropriation by painting and film, the latter an ideal medium for the fluidity Bersani discusses, better illustrates its appeal to modernists. In the hands of major artists and film directors, images that distil Brontë's meanings can be recovered and pressed into a dynamic similar to her own. The simultaneous assertion of sameness and difference, fusion and separation, so integral to *Wuthering Heights*, becomes part of a process in which the artist signifies kinship with the original and yet translates it into a new mode of expression. The visual emphasis thus goes beyond the written word that Brontë's characters themselves found too confining and limiting.

In a 1937 painting by Balthus (born Balthasar Klossowski) called "Les Enfants," which the artist gave to Picasso, who in turn donated it to the Louvre Museum, a boy and a girl are facing in opposite directions, he kneeling on a chair, with his elbow on a bare table, while she, her face turned to the viewer, kneels on the floor in the forefront, fully engrossed in the reading of a flattened book, the text of which seems blanked by the light. The boy wears a French schoolboy's smock; its drab, dark contours are repeated by a bag of coal beyond the table. The girl's attire is far more varied: a striped blouse, a sleeveless jersey, a black belt, a checkered skirt. She is feminine, erotic, her sexual appeal, accentuated by her bare long legs. The boy, by way of contrast, seems asexual in his dark drabness; his gaze into the distance thus counters that of any viewer forced, by the painting's composition, to rest on the figure of the prone girl. The contrast the pair presents thus is startling, mildly disturbing. Each child seems entranced by some alternative to the stark and somber interior which resembles a prison cell. But the girl, so rapt in the contemplation of the light surface of the book before her, seems superior to the boy who stares vacantly into the darkness.

No viewer stumbling upon this painting in the Louvre would automatically grasp that what Balthus has entitled "Les enfants – Hubert et Thérèse Blanchard" offers a representation other than that of the children named in the title. Yet the painting is an elaborate transformation of the second of fourteen pen-and-ink illustrations for *Wuthering Heights* which Balthus had begun in 1932 and completed in 1934–5, after he recovered from the adverse reaction to the first one-man exhibit of his unconventional paintings. In the corresponding drawing (now in a private collection), the children are attired in the proper historical costume; the boy Heathcliff is not staring away but also looking at the viewer; and the girl Catherine is not reading but in the act of writing, with pen in hand and an ink-well before her. The composition of the figures is otherwise identical, except that the boy's knee is closer to the girl's bent back, so much so that he seems to be pressing her down. There is no coal bag. The drawing is captioned, "I have got the time on [sic] with writing for twenty minutes."

Which of these versions is truer to its Brontëan original? Which captures more of *Wuthering Heights*? I would argue that the drawing that records the particular moment in which Catherine writes in her diary is, paradoxically, a much more limited rendering of the meanings embedded in *Wuthering*

Heights. Despite its modern setting and its reliance on the recognizable brother–sister pair of Hubert and Thérèse, the painting captures more of the book's meanings and also offers more insight into the artist's own relationship to those meanings. In the pen-and-ink drawings that relationship is quite overt: Balthus gives Heathcliff his own features and endows Catherine's with those of his future wife, from whom he was then temporarily separated. (She became a model for several other paintings, notably for "La Toilette de Cathy" [1933], a work in which Balthus also used an earlier illustration for *Wuthering Heights* to convey a distinctly personal – and angry – meaning.) In the painting of "Les Enfants," however, these relationships become richer, more fluid, and more universal.

The boy in "Les Enfants" is at once Hubert (another "H." double), Heathcliff, and Balthus (the artist who, like Heathcliff, goes by a single name). The girl is at once Thérèse, Catherine and Emily Brontë. Balthus undoubtedly recognized Brontë in the Catherine who authorizes herself by writing her diary. But by making the girl in the painting a reader rather than a writer, he actually introduces a more complicated statement about his own relationship to Brontë's art. The bright, blank pages that stand out so forcefully on the canvas are pages that can be covered with words or with drawings. The unfolded book may be a novel but it may also be a sketch-book such as artists use for their drawings and thumbnail studies. There is no need to impose the features of an adult artist on the somberly gazing boy. The belted smock the boy wears may be that worn in French schools, but it also makes him look monastic. The feminine girl, entranced by pages in a seemingly blank book appears to have reached, like Catherine, a stage her celibate counterpart has not yet attained. But since his smock also resembles that which painters have worn since the Middle Ages (when monks were artists) and since it is visually paralleled in the dark coal bag (charcoal being an artist's first tool in the gradual process of developing a painting), there is a sense that this uncouth boy may develop into an artist. He may be looking, in fact, for the images that are required to interpret this very moment in time at some later stage of his development.

What "Les Enfants" captures, then, is a dialectic as powerful as that on which *Wuthering Heights* is based. What is more, the painting adds one further relation to those already refracted and recombined through the Catherine/Heathcliff pairing: it also links Balthus to Emily Brontë, and thus establishes a connection between a male creator of visual images and a female creator of a verbal text. The two artists become, like Thérèse/Hubert, a brother–sister pair. Although the female is ahead in her psycho-social development, the coarser boy whose bent knee is above her supine body may revisit the "liminal" space they briefly share before their sundering in a reality governed by time. In this sense, he will master what she has mastered, even after she has been consumed by time. Did Balthus know that the prone girl, whose posture he obsessively repeats in many of his other paintings of female figures at the threshold of puberty, is assuming a stance that had been frequently adopted by a real-life Emily Brontë? Charlotte's staid friends remembered their surprise on finding Emily sprawling on the hearthrug or "habitually kneeling on the hearth, reading a book" (quoted by Gérin in her *Emily Brontë*). Among the "lax" traits with Charlotte transferred to Shirley Keeldar after her sister's death was, in fact, this uninhibited posture (*Shirley*, ch. 22).

In "Les Enfants" Balthus wonderfully condenses what required many pages of analytical prose in chapter 3 of this book. His painting converts an interpretation of *Wuthering Heights* into a personal act of homage. Emily Brontë read Percy Shelley's poem to Emilia Viviani as an utterance unconstrained by the limits of time and space. Shelley's "Epipsychidion," she felt, was as as much addressed to her − or more so − than to the flesh-and-blood woman in whom Shelley had become disenchanted. Balthus, who was designing the stage settings for Artaud's adaptations of Shelley's incest-drama *The Cenci* while working on his *Wuthering Heights* illustrations, similarly regards a long-dead author as his own epipsyche. On his canvas, his imagination can marry

Emily's. The reanimated ghost of a girl can be embraced by a modern artist with the same eagerness with which Heathcliff clasped the dead Catherine.

Luis Buñuel, the cinema's foremost surrealist, also embraced "el espíritu de Emilia Bronté" in his 1953 Mexican film, *Abismos de Pasión*. In a foreword to the movie he directed and wrote, Buñuel vows "to respect above all" the integrity of *Wuthering Heights*, intimating that he will be truer to it by far than the lavish 1939 Hollywood version by William Wyler. The film bears out his claim. Relying on Jorge Mistral and Irasema Dilian for roles associated with Laurence Olivier and Merle Oberon, Buñuel crafts a taut psychological drama that is as characteristically his as it is Brontëan. The film is not a historical costume drama. Set in what can pass as nineteenth-century rural Mexico or Spain, the characters could just as easily be transplanted into other places and other times. Despite its condensations, the film retains more than its American counterpart. Whereas the Hollywood version eliminates Hareton and Cathy altogether, much is made by Buñuel of the brutalization of a boy (here called Jorgito) who is the son of Hindley (here called Ricardo) at the Heights (which has become la Granja or Grange).

The child's victimization plays a central role. It contributes to the film's exploration of the uneasy proximity between sadism and affection, more fully exemplified by the hatred/love that binds Catalina (Catherine) and Alejandro (Heathcliff). When Hindley/Ricardo asks Hareton/Jorgito to stroke his face to help lull him into sleep, the boy complies, yet only after he has nervously glanced at a sharp knife nearby. Tenderness and cruelty are inseparable. The intensely disturbing moment in which a brutal father entrusts his life to the child he has tormented is not found in *Wuthering Heights*. But the incident nonetheless crystallizes something that seems as unmistakeably Brontëan as it is Buñuel's. In the book, Hindley's maltreatment of his own child helps to remind us of his brutality to the boy Heathcliff. Here, through Jorgito's wavering, we are meant to understand both the causes and the depths of Alejandro's hatred of Ricardo. And we are also reminded of its converse: Ricardo has vowed to kill Alejandro as soon as the usurper falls asleep.

Hindley does not carry out his aborted attempt to kill Heathcliff, but Buñuel's Ricardo does succeed after his first failure. In what is the director's major departure from a text he has otherwise fully "respected," the film that began with a gun-shot fired by Catalina/Catherine ends with her brother's shooting of Alejandro/Heathcliff. As the strains of Wagner's "Tristan und Isolde" mount in the background, Buñuel grants his lovers a bitterly ironic *liebestod*. Alejandro has crawled into the catacomb containing the recently buried Catalina. With blood pouring from the wound he has received, he deliriously embraces her corpse. Turning around, he sees her diaphanous ghost coming towards him. Extending his arms in an ecstatic gesture of welcome, he is felled by a second shot. The figure he perceived as a sister/bride turns out to have been that of their vengeful brother, the bearded Ricardo. Like Heathcliff, Alejandro sees the object of his desire in everything. (Heathcliff had complained that Catherine's "image" began to blend with the "most ordinary faces of men and women" – even with "my own features," mocking him "with a resemblance.") The idea to have Heathcliff killed by the brother whose eyes and Catherine's are so alike is one the novel may have suggested to Buñuel, who uses it to intensify the ironies of the film.

Such intensifications make *Abismos de Pasión* more overtly satirical than *Wuthering Heights*. Nonetheless, these and other changes, like the addition of boiled frogs, slaughtered pigs, a fly devoured by a spider (the Buñuel trademarks that go back to his first surrealist film with Salvador Dali), seem in keeping with his avowed faithfulness to the novel he has appropriated. For his purposes and those of "Emilia Bronté," he contends, are the same. Like the novelist, he wants to render the actions of "seres únicos para los que no existen las llamadas conveniencias sociales" [beings unique in their freedom from so-called conventions]. Buñuel allows Eduardo (Edgar) to raise the child whose birth killed Catalina (a boy, significantly, rather than a girl). But the pseudo-rationalism of this civilized and conventional man is what Buñuel's Brontë is asked to help him oppose. Her ferocity is the director's agent and ally.

What happens, however, when civilization itself embraces irrationalism? The question is raised by another film, which will be our last sample, properly so, since, as the most recent, it is also the most layered: a film based on a novel which is itself based on fictions enlisting *Wuthering Heights*, which is itself based on earlier Romantic fictions. In an essay mentioned before, Q. D. Leavis connects the "challenging modernity" of *Wuthering Heights* to Henri-Pierre Roché's *Jules and Jim* (1953), a novel François Truffaut reworked into the 1961 film of the same title (remade once more by Paul Mazursky in the 1980 *Willie and Phil* as a tribute to Truffaut).

Like Buñuel's Catalina, the Catherine who is Truffaut's heroine (called Kate in Roché's book) is an amoralist. Like Catherine Earnshaw, she oscillates between two lovers, Jules and Jim, versions of Edgar and Heathcliff. As Leavis shows, the two men enlist their common desire for the woman they share in order to bond with each other (as Lawrence's Gerald and Birkin unsuccessfully try to do). But Truffaut's quiet irony, so much more subdued than Buñuel's, invalidates the desire that binds this triangle of Romantics. The irrationality on which they pride themselves as they defy social conventions is becoming conventional, adopted by society at large. Instead of opposing civilization, they are therefore only mirroring its course. Brontë's Catherine/Heathcliff chose anarchy to maintain their distinctness. Truffaut's Catherine deforms Jules/Jim into potential clones of an anarchy found in the world at large.

Just as the multiple characters whose name began with "H." can confuse the reader of *Wuthering Heights*, so does the viewer of *Jules et Jim* strain to remember at times who is "Jules" and who is "Jim." We must resort to our visual memory of the actors to separate these brother Tweedles. Oskar Werner's doleful face must be recalled to help us

establish him as the Edgar-like humanist who survives to raise
two little daughters (a Brontëan father-caretaker of sisters
without a mother). Henri Serre, then, by elimination, must be
Jim, more passionate and intemperate. He, a Frenchman, will
be chosen by Catherine (Jeanne Moreau) when she forces him
to drown with her in an abrupt climax in which Maggie
Tulliver and Gudrun Brangwen blend with Catherine Earnshaw. But our difficulty in separating an Edgar from a
Heathcliff is important. For all their differences, they are
fellow-Romantics. They share a Bohemian youth, a contempt
for "so-called social conventions," and, above all, they share
Catherine, the Romantic *femme fatale.*

The ending of *Jules and Jim*, however, confers a further
meaning to the "J" of a shared *jeunesse*, a desire for eternal
youth. In the film's last moments we are jolted into
remembering the historical moment all three characters –
and we, along with them – have vainly tried to set aside. As
Jules, the gentle Austrian humanist, sadly watches the coffins
of Catherine and Jim disappear in the oven in which they are
incinerated, Nazi book-burnings and fascist riots, observed
by Jules with the same doleful expression, flash into their full
meaning. The image of the coffins sliding into the flames of
a crematorium on a slow, mechanical conveyor belt suddenly
becomes familiar. Our hindsight, from our own memory of
newsreels, evokes a "relation" to the real world to which
these lovers have not felt bound. Jules and Jim had bravely
fought (though on opposite sides) in the first World War. Sardonically, Truffaut reminds us that new flames will soon
erupt in an orgy of purification. Romantic transcendence, the
desire for a better order, will infect civilization itself and
create unforeseen convulsions. A death-wish does not need to
be confined to the lonely and the unique. Lockwood may be
inferior to the rarefied Catherine and Heathcliff, enveloped in
the haze of moors, roaming as eternal emblems of Romantic
desire. But Jules, who, like Lockwood, walks away from a
graveyard at the end, possesses a hindsight which the
"wuthering" of the second World War is about to confirm.
The romantic Jules who was Jim who is Catherine who was

Jules who had been Jim looks at ashes and smoke. As a withered grandchild of Brontë's Romantic creatures, he knows, unlike Lockwood, that their ghosts remain unquiet and disquieting − profoundly so.

Guide to further reading

Although the text of the Norton Critical Edition is hardly "authoritative," it seems more satisfactory than rival editions; moreover, the inclusion of contemporary reviews and nine critical essays is valuable (three of the essays from the 1963 edition have been replaced by other choices in 1972). There are other collections of essays and reviews: Miriam Allott, *Emily Brontë: Wuthering Heights, A Casebook* (London: Macmillan and Co., 1970); Richard Lettis and William E. Morris, *A Wuthering Heights Handbook* (New York: Odyssey Press, 1961); Thomas Vogler, *Twentieth-Century Interpretations of Wuthering Heights* (Englewood Cliffs, N.J.: Prentice-Hall, 1968). The fullest collection of reviews and early estimates of *Wuthering Heights* and the Bell "brothers" has been assembled by Miriam Allott in *The Brontës: The Critical Heritage* (London: Routledge and Kegan Paul, 1974). Although their literary assessments are of little value, there is much that is useful in Barbara and Gareth Lloyd Evans *The Scribner Companion to the Brontës* (1982; published in Great Britain by J. M. Dent and Sons as *Everyman's Companion to the Brontës*): an extraordinarily detailed "Calendar of Events," an overview of "Gondal," a glossary of difficult words (including West Yorkshire dialect), a list of characters (which even names all eight dogs at the Heights and Grange), and a topography.

Though it is doubtful that Emily Brontë intended to arrange her poems according to a "design comparable to the clear-cut blueprint of *Wuthering Heights*," the reader interested in her verses may want to inspect both C. W. Hatfield's edition of *The Complete Poems of Emily Jane Brontë* (New York: Columbia University Press, 1941), which contains a sugggested arrangement of them "as an Epic of Gondal," as well as Fannie E. Ratchford's fuller *Gondal's Queen: A Novel in Verse* (New York: Mc-Graw Hill, 1964). For those wanting further refinements, W. D. Paden, *An Investigation of Gondal* (New York: Bookman Associates, 1958), seems the obvious next step.

The issues of the *Brontë Society Transactions* are worth perusing; the journal contains a considerable number of interesting notes and assessments.

Biography

As the last in her cycle of biographies of Anne, Branwell, and Charlotte Brontë, Winifred Gérin's *Emily Brontë* (Oxford: Clarendon, 1971) seems tighter and more self-assured. By approaching the writer from different angles, Edward Chitham, *A Life of Emily Brontë* (Oxford and New York: Basil Blackwell, 1987) provides a valuable complement. Taken together, the two biographies furnish as rounded a portrait as we will ever get; they lay to rest all lingering notions about Emily's unworldliness. Though superseded by Gérin and Chitham, Muriel Spark's and Derek Stanford's *Emily Brontë: Her Life and Work* (London: Peter Owen, 1960) is still worth reading for insights into the growing legend of Emily as the inscrutable "sphinx of modern literature." A pleasing visual supplement can be found in Brian Wilks, *The Brontës: An Illustrated Biography* (New York: Peter Bedrick, 1986); the reproductions of Brontëana (especially the sketches and paintings by the four young artists) often are more telling than the text.

Critical studies

The prejudice against *Wuthering Heights* as a "crude" production lingered despite admirers and defenders such as A. C. Swinburne, whose 1883 *Athenaeum* essay (reprinted in his 1886 *Miscellanies*) unabashedly ranked the novel with the landmarks of Jacobean drama. In "*Jane Eyre* and *Wuthering Heights*," reprinted in her 1925 *The Common Reader*, Virginia Woolf adduced Emily Brontë's poetic imagination to argue that hers was (like Woolf's own fiction) a lyrical novel: "She could free life from its dependence on facts." But it was another member of the Bloomsbury group, C. P. Sanger, who finally turned the tide in Emily's favor by adopting, ironically enough, an approach opposite to Woolf's. In his 1926 Hogarth Press monograph, *The Structure of Wuthering Heights* (reprinted in all the collections cited above), Sanger irrefutably proved Emily Brontë's command of the actual world of fact by a detailed look at her chronological accuracy and her grip of laws of entail. The emphasis began to shift, aided no doubt by the kinship between *Wuthering Heights* and modernist structures of meaning, discussed above. Emily's artistic superiority to Charlotte now began to be asserted with increasing confidence, notably by Lord David Cecil in his *Early Victorian Novelists* (1935). Only with the recent advent of feminist criticism has Charlotte Brontë's work regained its former pre-eminence.

Thus, whereas from *c.* 1930 to 1970, the critical focus on *Wuthering Heights* diverted attention from Charlotte Brontë's books, the emphasis in the 1970s and 1980s has perceptibly shifted by giving primacy to *Jane Eyre, Villette, Shirley*, and, quite recently, even to Anne's two novels. This is not to say that Emily Brontë's novel has somehow resisted feminist analysis. Nina Auerbach's interest in the "demonic," for instance, has made the book central to her investigations in *Woman and the Demon: The Life of a Victorian Myth* (Cambridge, Mass.: Harvard University Press, 1982). But the absence of *Wuthering Heights* in Auerbach's earlier study of fictive "communities of women" seems as telling as its subordinate role in Sandra Gilbert's and Susan Gubar's *The Madwoman in the Attic* (New Haven and London: Yale University Press, 1979). There, the sixty pages devoted to "Emily Brontë's Bible of Hell" (in which she is linked to a male poet like Blake) are followed by 130 pages devoted to the sister-novelist whose "madwoman" provides the authors with their central icon. Other attempts to confront Emily Brontë's concern with gender-division and patriarchal power abound; but her ambivalence often seems frustrating to critics eager to detach a univocal ideology.

By far the best of such "ideological" readings is James H. Kavanaugh's *Emily Brontë* (Oxford: Basil Blackwell, 1985), which fruitfully enlists feminist, Marxist, and Lacanian coordinates for its reading of *Wuthering Heights*. The specialized terms on which the author rather relentlessly insists (and just as relentlessly glosses in explanatory footnotes) do not distract from his genuine insights into the novel. His "materialist" reading remains more sophisticated than that of earlier critics such as Arnold Kettle, or even Terry Eagleton, on whose discussion of the book as a battleground between "social" and "metaphysical" realities in *Myths of Power: A Marxist Study of the Brontës* (London: Macmillan, 1975) Kavanaugh intelligently builds.

Despite the abundance of superior critical articles − or chapters in studies such as Eagleton's, or Gilbert's and Gubar's, where Emily Brontë's work seems distinctly subordinated to Charlotte's − there are rather few critical books solely devoted to the poems and *Wuthering Heights*. Of these, besides Kavanaugh's work, Mary Visick's *The Genesis of 'Wuthering Heights'* (Hong Kong: Hong Kong University Press, 1958) is still worth perusing in its entirety, though salient excerpts are reprinted in the Norton critical edition and the other collections mentioned above. A few discussions not gathered in these anthologies might be mentioned here, not because they are the only such pieces worth citing, but rather because they engage topics I have raised in the course of this book.

Among the articles in journals, James R. Kincaid's "Coherent Readers, Incoherent Texts," *Critical Inquiry* 3 (1977), and Frank Kermode's "A Modern Way with the Classic," *New Literary History* 5 (1973), valuably enlist *Wuthering Heights* to raise important questions about the acts of reading and interpretation. Though

Guide to further reading

Kincaid devotes less pages to the novel *per se* than does Kermode, who offers his own reading to test traditional views of "what is 'timeless' in a classic," Kincaid's brilliant challenge to the arbitrary patterns we impose on a novel that insists on "a pattern of diverse and conflicting coherences" relies on no less than four contrary readings. Michael Macovski's "*Wuthering Heights* and the Rhetoric of Interpretation," *ELH* 54 (1987) extends Kincaid's approach by examining how Brontë uses audition in the novel itself in order to dramatize "the epistemological chasm between listeners and auditors." John E. Jordan's "The Ironic Vision of Emily Brontë," *NCF* 20 (1965) offers a sustained look at the novelist's artistry as a comic writer. Jonathan Wordsworth's "Wordsworth and the Poetry of Emily Brontë," *Brontë Society Transactions* 16 (1972), considers affinities that could profitably be further extended to *Wuthering Heights*, while Margaret Homans, who connects Dorothy Wordsworth to Emily Brontë's poetry in her *Women Writers and Poetic Identity* (Princeton: Princeton University Press, 1980), discusses the Wordsworthian figuration of nature in *Wuthering Heights* in "Repression and Sublimation of Nature in *Wuthering Heights*," *PMLA* 93 (1978). Lastly, N. M. Jacobs in "Gendered and Layered Narrative in *Wuthering Heights* and *The Tenant of Wildfell Hall*," *JNT* 16 (1986), though ignoring the dialogue between Anne and Emily, sets the two books in fruitful opposition.

Among the many discussions of *Wuthering Heights* in the framework of book-length studies, only a few of special interest to readers of this book will be cited. Though excerpted in the Norton edition, Dorothy Van Ghent's entire chapter on the book in *The English Novel: Form and Function* (New York: 1953) deserves to be consulted. Leo Bersani's *A Future for Astyanax: Character and Desire in Literature* (Boston: Little, Brown and Co., 1976) has also been noted above. Steven Cohan enlists the novel's treatment of "lost innocence" and maturation in the opening chapter of *Violation and Repair in the English Novel: The Paradigm of Experience from Richardson to Woolf* (Detroit: Wayne State University Press, 1986); his careful contrasts between *Wuthering Heights* and earlier and later fictions, such as *Clarissa* and *Tess of the D'Urbervilles*, are valuable. The resistance of *Wuthering Heights* to definitive interpretations is linked to its use of repetition by J. Hillis Miller in *Fiction and Repetition: Seven English Novels* (Cambridge, Mass.: Harvard University Press, 1982). Finally, though strong, the discussions of *Wuthering Heights* in both Robert Kieley's *The Romantic Novel in England* (Cambridge, Mass.: Harvard University Press, 1972) and U. C. Knoepflmacher's *Laughter and Despair: Readings in Ten Novels of the Victorian Era* (Berkeley and London: University of California Press, 1971) are less important for their own sake than for their placement within the wider continuum each author traces.

Index

Absalom, 87
adolescence: viii, 16, 80; and
  dreaming, 115; Keats on,
  viii–x; Rousseau on, xviii
Allott, Miriam, 128
Amnon, 87
Arnold, Matthew: 30, 106,
  108–109; "Haworth Churchyard," 114–15
Artaud, Antonin, 122
Auerbach, Nina, *Woman and
  the Demon*, 130

Balthus (Balthaser Klossowksi):
  WORKS: "Les Enfants,"
  xviii, 119–23; "La Toilette
  de Cathy," 121
Barrett Browning, Elizabeth, 2,
  30
Bersani, Leo, *A Future for
  Astyanax*, 119, 131
Bible, the: 103; references to:
  Kings, 85; *Matthew*, 85–86,
  88; *Samuel*, 87
*Blackwood's Edinburgh Maga-
  zine*, read by the Brontës,
  28–29, 30
Blake, William, xv, xvii, 81,
  83, 88, 106, 130
Blanchard, Hubert and Therese.
  See Balthus, "Les Enfants"
Bradner, Leicester, 29
Branwell, Elizabeth, 72, 81, 92
"The Bridegroom of Barna"
  (anon.), 29
Briggs, Charles, 31

Brontë, Anne, xvii, 92–94
  passim, 102–3, 105, 130;
  Charlotte Brontë on, 2, 3, 4,
  110–11. WORKS: *Agnes
  Grey*, 1, 4, 11; *The Tenant of
  Wildfell Hall*, 1; as response
  to *Wuthering Heights*, xvii,
  4, 109–11, 131.
Brontë, Branwell: *See* Brontë,
  Patrick Branwell
Brontë, Charlotte, x–xvii *passim*, 1–11 *passim*, 93–94,
  103, 130; on Anne Brontë,
  2, 3, 4, 110–11; rejects
  Branwell, 99, 111; sees Emily as former self, 111–12;
  on Emily's temperament, xii,
  3, 113; lacks Emily's grasp
  of male psychology, 100; as
  editor of *Wuthering Heights*,
  1–2, 5, 108, 112.

  Works:

  "Biographical Notice of Ellis
  and Acton Bell," 3–5, 23,
  29, 98, 99, 110–11
  "Editor's Preface to *Wuthering
  Heights*," x–xvii *passim*,
  5–10, 11, 28, 80, 111–13,
  115, 119; its Lockwoodian
  diction, xi, 9–10, 112; and
  Mary Shelley's Preface to
  Frankenstein, 9
  Jane Eyre, xi, 1, 3, 7, 111–12;
  contrasted to *Wuthering
  Heights*, xi, xvi, 94, 97–98

.